20½ Ways For A Woman to Please Her Man
(and keep him)

Produced and Published By
You Are Loved Publishing, copyright © 2011
www.youarelovedpublishing.com

20½ Ways For A Woman to Please Her Man (and keep him)

Distributed, Produced and Published By
You Are Loved Publishing,

First Printing: July 2011

ISBN 978-1451543759

The examples used in this book of individuals are drawn from the writer's experience. All names are fictional and any resemblance to any person(s) who have these names in real life is entirely coincidental.

DEDICATION

This book is dedicated to Trenna, a vision of perfected love in my life. Thank you for being in my world and sharing with me your uniqueness and passion for the things of God. If I had the privilege of designing a woman for me, I could not have created a woman more beautiful and precious as you. You are the epitome of what a woman should be, how she can be used by God to enhance the man God gives her and how she should love those who He places in her life. The iconic symbol in this book is a flower and it represents the way you have blossomed into a full blown representation of love that has thoroughly pleased me. I love you unconditionally.

Thank you, Boo!

DEDICATION

This book is dedicated to Trenna, a vision of perfected love in my life. Thank you for being in my world and sharing with me your uniqueness and passion for the things of God. If I had the privilege of designing a woman for me, I could not have created a woman more beautiful and precious as you. You are the epitome of what a woman should be, how she can be used by God to enhance the man God gives her and how she should love those who He places in her life. The iconic symbol in this book is a flower and it represents the way you have blossomed into a full blown representation of love that has thoroughly pleased me. I love you unconditionally.

Thank you, Boo!

Table of Contents

INTRODUCTION

Flowers... are a proud assertion that a ray of beauty out values all the utilities of the world.

~Ralph Waldo Emerson, 1844

You have the power to make your relationship great. This book gives you at least 20 ½ tools to do it. It is written by a male (yours truly) and it conveys the MVP (male point of view). Let me say one more time before you get into the reading that this book will at times feel and sound like it is written all about him and that would be accurate. This is a book all about your man and the more you read the more you can get into his brain.

The subtitle of the book says, "and keep him." This is in no way a suggestion that you are totally responsible for the success and happiness in your marriage. What it is meant to imply is as a man, I believe every man would be happy to have a wife who follows these suggestions with consistency and sincerity. No one person can be held responsible for the longevity of a marriage. People have different quirks, backgrounds, ideologies, and even mental illness that can contribute to the deterioration of even the best potential relationships.

Dr. Rodney Pearson

Without understanding some basic gender differences your relationship can really suffer. We will explore how a woman can better understand how her man thinks and how he sees her. It may cover some things you already know and reveal some things you don't. Some things you may do very well and for other things you may need a little help. I hope you find the help you need as you absorb and refer back to the information you get in this book.

If you feel your relationship is falling apart, then you are doing the right thing by reading this book. If you have made the lifelong commitment to cherish and honor your relationship, then you deserve to be happy. If you merely want to refresh your relationship, this is the right book for you too!

20 ½ Ways for a Woman to Please Her Man, is all about helping you, as a woman, make your relationship with your man more pleasurable, and, consequently, longer lasting. The knowledge that you gain from this book coupled with your willingness to adjust your thinking and patterns of behavior that are harmful to your relationship are essential. This book takes a realistic and positive look at the differences that hold many women down and the conflicts that exist in many relationships.

Although it is primarily written for the heterosexual married woman and women who hope to be married, you will see that many of the principles can also be applied to any relationship, be it intimate, platonic or even professional. In fact, any woman can benefit from the information in this book, as it gives the perfect guidelines for building a healthy and mutually fulfilling, intimate relationship. You will find the reading fun with some impactful, down-to-earth stories about real people. My hope is that you will read it and discuss the issues openly and honestly with your man. Certain topics may have to be revisited from time to time to refresh an understanding of issues and resolutions. Reference this book as often as possible to keep the lines of communications open and healthy.

It is designed for women who want to find the recipe to a real life fairytale relationship with a great man. You may be thinking, "I can't do this alone." You are right! You must have a willing partner, but you need as much knowledge and information as possible. So the theme of this book is about making your man happy with you. It was written to you and for you, and definitely not to your man. It is to help you understand how he thinks and what he thinks of you. It's not designed to help him. I repeat with emphasis, this book is not designed to help him! It is knowledge you need most, because it was probably never taught to you.

Now let me be real and say that what you will learn is not an instant cure for every problem relationship. Even after you have read every chapter it will take time to change harmful patterns of behavior. For instance, if you've been jealous or controlling, it may take a while to change these types of behaviors, but the following chapters, you will act as a resource you can go back to and draw from during your journey to wholeness.

Many women don't feel that they need any help loving their men, because God designed women to love. It is true most women love hard and deep. They sometimes get overwhelmed and even lose control because of the intensity of their love. They totally understand and practice dedication and devotion to the fullest and often feel that this innate trait and natural ability to love is enough to keep their men happy, but you need to understand that it is not. With nearly 70% of marriages ending in divorce today, we must conclude that something is not right with the way we love. You can blame it all on men or the dysfunctionality of our society, but there is a part of this alarming statistic for which women must also take responsibility.

WARNING: THIS BOOK IS NOT ABOUT PLEASING YOU. READ WITH EXTREME CAUTION! As you learn more about the deeper needs of your man, execute the suggestions and develop the methods given to you. I pray in turn he will want to please you even more, so read carefully. Underline words and phrases that you connect to. Be open to changes you may have to make that will make you a better mate for him. Whatever you do to enhance your relationship will ultimately make you a happier woman. The process will not happen overnight, but with patience and consistency you will have the best chance possible for a fulfilling and happy relationship. You should both find mutual benefits and pleasure by working on this together. May God's blessing ever be upon you as you seek to be the best woman you can be, firstly, for yourself and, secondly, for the man of your dreams forever! There are a few points I'd like to cover before we get into the 20 ½ ways to please your man.

"Man" Basics

Let me say on the onset that I am not an expert on women, but I am an expert on men. I have been one for over half a century and loved every step of the way. Maybe not an adult man all of this time, but indeed a man in process. From the day I was born I was being influenced and developed as a man, as is the case for most men. Frankly, the first thing put in our mouths, our only fully functional apparatus, is a woman's breast. The first thing we see when our eyes start working is a woman's eyes, her loving smile and then, of course, those loving ample breasts. We hear her sweet, soft voice in our ears that soothe our fears of the unfamiliar world we suddenly arrived in. We feel her soft hands caress our little bodies as she washes us. These of course are lasting memories of a mother's love that eventually aid in our growing sexuality. Our loving mothers aggressively seek to please us and keep us pleased as any mother should. For the young "pre-man" these memories also become a part of our attraction to our ultimate mate and bride. We look for all of these same features in a woman, but now from a matured perspective. We were created like this and will develop from this place of origin and we, normally, progress into your average grown man.

Most women never connect these points and may not see the importance of why I bring it up, but this is the origin of your husband's attraction to you. The root of understanding your man starts by looking at his relationship with his mother. His mother is his first love and how he loves his mother has a lot to do with how he loves you. Ok, enough said about this without sliding into Greek mythology.

Damaged Goods

I was once in a relationship with a woman who was beautiful, sincere and with a vibrant personality. At first, she seemed to be exactly what I wanted and needed in a woman. She said that I was everything she wanted, and I was anxious to marry her. It wasn't long before the truth behind her gorgeous smile was revealed to me. The young lady had been brutally abused by her father for years. She was filled with mistrust and her thinking was skewed and twisted as to how an intimate relationship with a man should be. All of her previous relationships had been short lived according to her account; it seemed as if they were destined for doom from the beginning. When our relationship ended, she made a statement in response to my last effort to resolve our differences. From an offended position, she spewed from her lips these words, "You talk to me as if I am damaged goods." My response which insulted her even more was probably *the straw that broke the camel's back* and brought the final end to our status as a couple. I said to her, "I think you must deal with your damage before you will ever have a fulfilling relationship with anyone."

Most people, women and men alike, don't realize the extent of the damage they may have suffered from unhealthy relationships, a dysfunctional childhood, or past abuse of any kind. One of the reasons for this is that the emotional pain from the memories alone is often so intense that they are more easily avoided than dealt with. This lack of resolution and healing leaves the person volatile and ill-equipped to deal with the pressures and unexpected irregularities that occur in even the most normal of potentially healthy relationships. This means that before you can start to understand your man, you must be aware of your own mental and emotional condition.

In order for this book to be effective, you must ask yourself this question, "Have I given reasonable attention to my own past hurts?" If you can honestly answer, "Yes," you have a better chance of having a mutually fulfilling relationship. If the answer is, "No," I would advise you to give careful consideration to these unresolved issues as quickly as possible. When you filter new pains through past hurts sometimes the impact is much more devastating than the original hurt. It's like breaking the same bone at the same place again. After multiple hurts some people just become numb.

If you've been violated, abused or a victim of unresolved trauma, please get some help to work through those issues before you try to enter into a new relationship if possible. This may mean pursuing other self-help reading materials such as this book, attending seminars and or workshops, or even receiving therapeutic help from a qualified professional such as a counselor or minister. This doesn't mean that you are crazy; it simply means that the damage that has been done to you emotionally and mentally may take more time and effort to heal than you may have estimated.

Your own healthy emotional state of being is an essential piece that cannot be ignored or overlooked if you really want the best relationship possible. You must be willing to be honest and open about yourself. By this I mean, you cannot place the blame on everyone else and avoid taking responsibility for the part you have played in spoiled past relationships. These relationships may have failed due in part to your damaged status, but you cannot ignore the fact that you were an active participant. Due to past damage, you must stay open to the idea that everything that you have learned or felt about past relationships may need correction and/or adjustments. This is because everything that was filtered through or processed with faulty thinking may have heavily influenced the failures you have been experiencing or your viewpoints on the things you see and feel.

An example of the effects of working with damaged goods would be a person cooking a gourmet meal with all the beautiful garnishes, but using spoiled meat. Even if every other part of the meal is perfect, the spoiled meat makes the entire meal a disaster. Many women are guilty of spending too much time on the beautiful garnishing and accessories (like hair, makeup and clothes) while ignoring the spoiled meat (like attitude, fear and insecurity); thinking that no one will notice. The bottom line is that you must deal with the damaged goods. This may initially result in feeling the hurt of the past you've tried to avoid. But in order to get healing, this may be unavoidable. Whatever you do, you cannot assume the position of the proverbial ostrich with his head in the sand; hoping it will just all go away. Without dealing with these issues, they will come back to haunt you when you least expect it.

You must also be aware of your man's "damaged goods." You may not know the full extent of his damage, but you cannot ignore the fact that his spiritual, mental and emotional state is an important part of your long term happiness. Women who are attracted to the wrong guys are usually ignoring one or all of the aforementioned states. They get caught up in his financial status or his good looks. They love his tone of voice or how he combs his hair. These things are nice, but you cannot build a long lasting, healthy relationship on them. The things in this book were written for enhancements and should be practiced by two people with reasonably good foundations to build on. If you are a semi-desperate and/or damaged woman, you should be extremely selective as to whom you allow to get close to you! In other words, don't trust your good feelings alone.

Spoiled Brat

Men should want to "spoil" their women in a positive way! By "spoil" I mean that they should want them to feel special and entitled, but if he has taken it too far, he may have problems, especially if you are not "spoiling" him in return. If you feel you deserve to be treated like a queen, that is fine, but do you treat your man like a king? Do you even know how? Have you ever been taught how a man wants to be treated or are you using your own ideas that may or may not be correct. If you come into the relationship making demands, because you are accustomed to men putting you up on a pedestal, you may quickly be very disappointed. Some women go from relationship to relationship looking for a man who will treat them a certain way, put up with all her issues and provide at least her basic needs. This sounds reasonable, but if your expectations are higher than your man's ability to meet them, you could be putting him in an unfair position. This unfair position he is in may not be because he is a bad guy at all.

Being a spoiled brat may make you feel powerful and confident, but it could also destroy your chances of having a healthy relationship, if you don't have people around you to help keep your attitude in check and balance your expectations. Listen to the good advice from people who are loving (and brave) enough to tell you the truth about yourself. Then you have to really be willing to make an honest attempt to change. Changing won't be easy!

Good Communication

One of the major things you will get from this book is the importance of knowing how to communicate with your man.

Men do not read minds and in most cases they do not read or understand feelings! Have you ever noticed that when a man sees a woman crying they always ask the same question, "What's wrong?" When most women see another woman crying, they start crying too! We just don't get this! Men eventually stop assuming anything when it comes to women because they are often wrong in whatever they assume. In this book you will find that much of your relationship will be about good communication with your man. Most men are at a loss when it comes to communicating with women, because of what they see as the shifting of women's emotions and lack of continuity. When women speak in frustration they usually leave their man behind, because she is so tapped into her feelings, which may be all over the place. The man is looking for the logic and the feelings just complicate things for him. As you read this book you may start to understand his line of thinking and hopefully develop better communication skills.

A More Excellent Way

Another resource that can aid tremendously in the repairing of damaged goods is a focus on spiritual essentials. I am a pastor of a nondenominational Christian church, and, although this book was not written for Christians, it was written by a Christian. You will read several references to sayings and writings that come from the Bible. As with many ancient writings, truth is truth no matter how long ago it may have first been penned. I believe that we are all mind, body and spirit. We cannot deal with the principles necessary for a healthy relationship with your man and ignore the spiritual aspects of your being.

There is nothing more healing for you than to be connected to your creator in a fully functional and intelligent relationship. The Bible is full of wisdom and advice for a woman who wants to know how to please her man. The number one spiritual component for any relationship is LOVE. While some people see love as a good feeling, I must agree with the Bible that says in 1 John 4:7-8 that, "God is love." If God is love as the Bible says, then real love is spiritual and not limited to just a good feeling. There are many things that can feel good that are far from love. Sleep can be a good feeling. Eating can generate good feelings. A new house or car can make you feel good, but none of these things is love. A relationship built on true unconditional love is the most fulfilling relationship a person can have. I hope the things you learn in this book will help you deal with some of the blockers that can get in the way, and help you avoid counterfeit love, which is further addressed in the chapter entitled, "Love Your Man Unconditionally."

For All You Seasoned Veterans

I know that some of you have a "Been There, Done That" badge of honor on your chest. You're not new to pleasing a man or you've been around long enough that you have a few notches on your belt. You may have the curse of "set in my ways" on you and that might ruin any chance you have of building a healthy relationship. You may feel that you're too old to try or learn some new tricks. Let me admonish you now. In order for this book to help you at all you may need to allow your old ways to be challenged a bit. I know several women who entered into relationships in their mid-30s to early 40s and even older and the struggle was not with their man, it was with themselves. They may have had expectations that were unrealistic, they didn't want to change and/or they misunderstood the intentions of their man as they compared him to others and even to themselves. You would probably be the first one to tell a new bride that she must be flexible if she wants her marriage to last. Make sure you are listening to that advice for yourself.

You may have been a raving beauty at one point, but today you look in the mirror and you don't see that woman anymore. Don't allow yourself to become bitter, because your looks have changed. It just means that you must compensate for the lack of outward beauty with more inward beauty. The inward beauty can last as long as you live while the outer beauty will surely fade away. My wife was 49 years old when we met, and, although she was an attractive woman, it was the glow I saw emanating from her gorgeous heart that drew me to her the most. My widowed mother is 78 years old and has a boyfriend. She is sweeter to her man than I have seen the way some women half her age treat their man!

So, remember you are only as old as you act and feel. Maybe you have little control of your feelings, but in most cases you are in full control of your actions. I've heard the phrase "growing old gracefully," but only after reaching 50 years old did I begin to understand what that meant. Keep your smile as long as you can. Be kind to other people. Don't complain and criticize everything that is not to your liking or standards. If you're already in a relationship you should know that your man wants to be happy and grow old gracefully with you, so you might as well do everything you can to make it as pleasant as possible for both of you.

Unconditional Love Story

In my book, *20 ½ Ways for a Man to Love His Woman*, I told the story of how I met my wife and I have decided to reprint the story in this book as well. I hope that our story will be as inspiring to you as it has been to so many others.

My wife, Trenna, is an incredible woman who has resurrected me from the dead after two failed marriages and a couple of years of being single. Both past marriages started with good intentions, but eventually became like a horror movie – *Frankenstein and His Bride-to-Be!* With the joy I now experience on a daily basis, this book has new meaning to me.

Here is our story:

Trenna and I met at a network marketing business briefing. She walked in without incident and sat in the back of the room. I didn't pay much attention to her. I was busy with matters of the meeting, as I was the main speaker. I had been married most of my adult life and was now single again after my second marriage of ten years ended nearly two years earlier. Needless to say, the life of dating and being single was not my preferred status.

At the end of the presentation, as the night progressed, Trenna was the winner of a prize for becoming a business associate. The prize was a book that highlighted successful tips in the business. Just as she stood to receive her gift, one of the business representatives suggested that the prize be given to another guest who was there and had signed up earlier that day. I was faced with a dilemma. I didn't want Trenna to be disappointed nor did I want to be embarrassed. So I said, "Okay then Trenna, I will give you one of the books I've written entitled *Significantly Single*. I will give you my number to call me with your address and I will be sure to send it to you." Everyone applauded and we continued with the meeting. Little did I know, that book would be our connection for life.

It was a pretty exciting time for me. In two days it was my birthday and I was leaving to go on a cruise to the Bahamas. I remembered thinking that I'd just continue in my search for my soul-mate. I met a beautiful young lady on the cruise, but it didn't result in a relationship at all. I came back home, went on a couple dates, but no one sparked my interest. Then, I met a young lady over the phone during a business transaction. She sounded fun, bright, and easy to talk to with a great personality. Though she lived in Atlanta, Georgia, we talked every day and night for weeks, and I just knew I had found "that girl." She had to be the woman I was looking for - my soul-mate!

Dr. Rodney Pearson

So, I decided to fly to Atlanta to meet her face to face. To my utter amazement the woman did not show up! There I was, sitting in the airport, waiting for hours not hearing from her, no emails, no calls, and no explanation. In fact, after that painful event, I never heard from her again. I left Atlanta disappointed, upset and confused. On the plane headed back home, I said to myself in disgust, "I am done and finished! I am no longer looking! I am going to be significantly single until God sends the right woman." I realized then, obviously *my* choices in the past had not been the best – surely God's will be better!

About five hours later back in Phoenix I called my business partner while I drove home from the airport. She told me upon leaving a business seminar, Trenna mentioned her disappointment about not getting the help she needed with her new business. My partner left the book I promised Trenna, with a friend who would make sure she got it.

As I pulled myself together from the great disappointment in Atlanta, I decided to focus on building my business, rather than looking for a new wife, and called Trenna. We arranged a meeting to help her get her new business started and running successfully. Trenna let me know she got the book, thanked me and agreed to meet the next day. Now remember, Trenna got the book, I made a new revelation to stop looking for a wife and we made the appointment to meet all on the same day, the Saturday I get back in town!

She hung up the phone and started reading the book. Unbeknownst to me, while reading the book, old hurts and emotions came up as she was confronted with her past decisions, failed marriages and relationships. She too wanted to be married and had multiple "test runs" in relationships with men who were surface and shallow. She wanted a relationship rooted in God, a man who was secure in himself; someone who would love her *and* her children. She had five children that were adults and living on their own, and an 8 year old living at home. Her major concern was her two boys who aspired to live the "gangsta rapper" lifestyle as hustlers and gang members. She loved her boys, but it seemed to her that their lives and issues constantly conflicted with hers and her chance of having a happy marriage.

In the book she read how she must accept her "singlehood" and stop basing her worth and self-esteem on being married. The book described situations that she was able to relate to and she painfully accepted her need to change her perspective and methods. Trenna said, in total surrender, she read the entire book. The reality and truth of her unhealthy behaviors as a single woman hit her like a ton of bricks that night. After reading the book, she was ready to change and start a new life as a *whole significantly single woman.*

The next day we met at my home, as planned, after church. I prepared a simple meal. We broke the ice with brief introductions and small talk on each other's background. As we continued talking, it caught us both off guard how easy and smooth our conversation was. It was as if we had known each other for years! We weren't trying to impress each other, nor had any hidden agendas. To our surprise, our backgrounds were similar. We found out that we both spent our teenage years in the same city, for a period of time, lived just a few blocks away from each other. We had an immediate connection! We discussed our past and concluded that our past relationships ended for most of the same reasons. For the rest of the day, we laughed together and almost cried together as we exposed our pains and fears.

When the meeting was over, we knew it was something special; but dared to attach a label of love to it for fear of falling into the same "love trap" we had experienced before and knew, all too well! We never got to the business we came together to discuss and decided to meet again. After two more meetings and no business, we had to question ourselves. I remember my ex-girlfriend asking me if I was interested in Trenna. I told her that I was not; I just wasn't sure of what was going on. It had only been three days and I just didn't know enough to know what I felt. It was that discussion with my former girlfriend that made me realize that Trenna was someone special and what I was feeling was not lust. It was not infatuation. It was not just a new challenge. It was different than anything I had ever encountered before in my life. She didn't have any resemblance to women I was typically attracted to. Although she was beautiful, I was able to resist her physical attractiveness. After all, looks had gotten me in trouble before, and I wasn't falling for that again anyway. What I did see was the beauty inside of her that shined like a glowing star. She had an innocent laugh and a precious smile that seemed to kindly whisper, "You can trust me." Though I hadn't touched her yet, I could feel her.

The following Saturday we had our first date. It was the most romantic date I had ever had; all we did was sit in my living room. We ate dinner and talked about everything under the sun. She loved talking as much as I did. There was no competition or power struggles. She was such an intelligent, gracious and classy woman. We talked about wanting a relationship that was not based on sex and material things. We talked and laughed the entire night away. For the next six weeks, we sought to see and talk with each other every day, every chance we got, and fell deeply in love. Without sexual intercourse, we experienced the deepest love I could ever imagine!

At the end of those six weeks, we could not hold back any longer and we were married. I would never suggest to anyone to do it that way, but for us it was what we had to do. Today, it has been over three years and without a single thought of divorce or separation. We love each other unconditionally and trust each other unselfishly. We are happy and we love being together. Every night we go to bed holding each other before falling asleep. We wake up greeting each other with "I love you." Although we both are in our fifties, we make love with the passion and vigor of our thirties regularly! We talk to each other several times a day on the phone and, although our lives are busy, we make time to be with each other, having lunch and dinner together as often as possible. We actually enjoy each other's company. Trenna is my best friend in the world! I don't like to travel without her and have turned down speaking engagements, if I couldn't take her with me. We share in everything we do. She has proven to be the best partner in business, ministry, family, and life I could have ever hoped for.

I often say, "I am glad God didn't give me what I prayed for when I asked for a wife." God gave me just what I needed. I would have been cheated if I had gotten anyone other than Trenna. She is more than a soul mate could ever be to me. I call her my "eternal-mate!" I wish that everyone could have the kind of marriage we share; there is no question in my mind that I will feel the same way twenty years from now. She will be my mate, my best friend, and my obsession until the day I die.

Let's Do it!

Well, you just read the longest *"Introduction"* I have ever written. I hope that the message is clear and you are ready to enter into this "man world!" Some things may seem a little confusing to you as you hear the way a man thinks, but it can help you if you see this book as a text book full of facts, examples and good advice. Take charge of the destiny of your relationship. With a strong and healthy love, you can create a legacy that will be a blessing to your family for years to come. May you grow in passion and amorous romance with your man, crossing the borders of reality and spilling over into a living fantasy as you explore true ecstasy with *20 ½ Ways for a Woman to Please Her Man!*

ONE

Don't Make Your Man Your Woman

This first chapter is a very important one to all you beautiful ladies, because it emphasis the difference between a man and a woman and why you as a woman should appreciate the "maleness" in your man. Let us begin by firmly saying that your man doesn't think like you and probably never will. You may think he should (although you shouldn't), but he never ever will. It isn't because he just wants to think differently, but because his brain is simply wired differently than a woman's and that is the way he is supposed to be.

The following is a rather comical email I received from my wife that was forwarded to her. The original writer is unknown and I had to do a little editing just to keep it clean, but it shows one viewpoint of the thinking of a typical male. Let me emphasis the term "typical male." There are exceptions to this "typicalness," but the email is a funny perspective of the average man. Here it is:

Choosing a Wife.

A man wanted to get married. He was having trouble choosing among thre e likely candidates. He gives each woman a present of $5,000 and watches to see what they do with the money.

The first does a total makeover. She goes to a fancy beauty salon, gets her h air done, new makeup; buys several new outfits and dresses up very nicely f or the man. She tells him that she has done this to be more attractive for hi m because she loves him so much.
The man was impressed.

The second goes shopping to buy the man gifts. She gets him a new set of go lf clubs, some new gizmos for his computer, and some expensive clothes. As she presents these gifts, she tells him that she has spent all the money on hi m because she loves him so much.
Again, the man is impressed.

The third invests the money in the stock market. She earns several times t he $5,000. She gives him back his $5,000 and reinvests the remainder in a joint account. She tells him that she wants to s ave for their future because she loves him so much.
Obviously, the man was impressed.

The man thought for a long time about what each woman had done with th e money he'd given them.

Then…he married the one with the biggest breasts.

One of the biggest problems that can exist in a relationship is when one expects the other to think like they think. Everybody has a different way of processing what they see, feel, hear or interpret what is going on around them. Any time a person judges someone else based on the way they would have done something they have made an unfair judgment. Our decisions are made based on our perception of the situation. Our perception can be influenced by so many things.

Men and women often perceive things through their unwritten "code of conduct." Let me give you an example. Many females maintain an unwritten rule or standard that says a real girlfriend should not date her ex-boyfriend or ex-husband. If she does she is considered a trader or worse. Most guys don't go by that standard at all, instead their unwritten rule is "let the best man win!" Similarly, when guys break up with a girl they can usually move to another girl fairly easy. Most females are highly insulted by this. They usually assume that if a guy does that it means he never loved her in the first place. For the male, moving on to another female is his way of closing out the old relationship. In many cases a guy will actually recommend an ex to a man they feel will treat her good. The man sees this as a compliment to her and knows he would only do this if he cared about her and wanted her to be with someone he trusted. The woman in most cases is appalled by this gesture. They feel that you are just passing them on like a piece of meat. It is a great insult to a woman and a gesture of friendship and respect in the eyes of most men. The reason for this is that if the man really cares about you he still wants to protect you. This is his way of showing his concern. I know all this may sound sick to you, but it is how many men think. He would rather you be with someone he knows, instead of you being on the open market and a target for predators.

I can remember being utterly confused by a woman I was dating when I was single. She wanted to break off our relationship which really hurt me. I licked my wounds for a couple of days. Then I finally went out on a date with a new woman. When my former girlfriend found out that I had gone out with someone else, she was so angry and viciously attacked me calling me a desperate two timer. I said to her, "But you are the one who broke up the relationship, I'm just trying to move on." Her response was, "You could at least wait until you're out of my system." I said, "How long is that supposed to be?" Well, that question made her even angrier and it made me completely confused. She later explained to me that she had broken up with me in her "head," but not yet in her heart. This is a foreign concept for most men. They are able to move on from a failed relationship much quicker than the average woman. As far as I was concerned, the head and the heart was the same thing. I was hurt, rejected and disappointed and being with another woman was the best way to start the healing process. Needless to say, many men think the same way I do.

Statistics suggest that after a divorce most men are in a serious new relationship in about a year, but it takes most women 2 to 3 years before they feel comfortable enough for a fully committed relationship. Men may begin casually dating right away. Most guys can see their former wives or girlfriends as friends fairly quickly. Most women want to sever all ties and have nothing to do with their ex's for eternity! Also, most guys can talk about their ex's and the things they did as a matter of fact, without emotions getting out of hand or developing a desire to return to the ex. For most women, if they hear a man talk about his ex it means he has not gotten over her yet.

These are just a few of the ways most men perceive relationships differently than most women. Now remember, I said "most." There will be exceptions to these standards and the circumstances may be different causing a different result, but these are basic standards. Let's talk about a few more ways that a man's perception may be different than a woman's.

Chris and Vicky

Chris and Vicky got into a big argument which almost caused their one year marriage to end. One hot summer day Vicky suggested that they go to the beach and have a little picnic and do some swimming. So they went to the local beach, spread out a blanket and a nice setting and begin to enjoy their day. As the day progressed Vicky became very annoyed at Chris as he looked at the girls who walked by. He wasn't gawking, but he was gazing. The girls were beautiful and it seemed as if it was bikini day because it seemed to be what every woman was wearing. Vicky could not understand why Chris seemed to look at every girl who walked by. Even if they were fully engaged in a conversation Chris would casually glance at the passing beach walkers. Finally, in an abrupt rage Vicky jumped up and began packing up the picnic spread.

On the way home Vicky was silent. Chris had no idea what was going on. For the fifth time he asked, "Baby, what's wrong?" She finally explained that she felt totally disrespected, because he was looking at the women at the beach as if she wasn't there. Chris was baffled. From his perspective he would have had to close his eyes completely in order to not see those women. They were unavoidable. From her point of view, she didn't expect him to totally ignore them, but she felt he was focused on them. In her mind, he desired to have every one of those women. Vicky had a lot to learn about her new husband and about men.

Is it fair for a man to accuse you of trying to entice other men if you have on a nice skirt and a pretty blouse? Your answer is probably "no." You would say that you just put on some nice clothes as you do every day. Well, if you have a shapely body most men are going to look at you whether you tried to entice them or not. Just because you want to look nice doesn't mean you want men to desire you sexually. In the same way, just because a man looks at a woman doesn't mean he desires her sexually. Men are visual and are naturally attracted to shapely hips and breasts. Even if a man has been happily married for years, it doesn't mean that another women's body doesn't draw his attention. He is created to be attracted to those body parts. Even if he doesn't know it intellectually, a man is attracted to a woman's hips, because he innately wants to reproduce. Hips represent the woman's ability to physically support and carry children in her womb which is the purpose of the difference between a man's and woman's pelvis.

Attraction to breasts is also due to the support of children. Accentuated breasts are like a billboard that says, "I'm ready for children." Thus the innate attraction that men have to big breasts may be more out of his control than you may think. He may not know it intellectually, but his body knows it. So it is a basic instinct of your man to desire to reproduce (which looks like he just wants to have sex) and be attracted to these body parts. Now with this in mind we clarify that it is not basic instinct for him to have sexual relationships with every woman he is attracted to. Nor is this license for him to gawk at beautiful women (we deal more about that as being disrespectful in *20 ½ Ways For a Man to Love His Woman*). That is a moral decision which he is very much in control of. Those morals are influenced by different things like culture, religion, laws, etc.

Body parts play a major part in attraction, but most people, men and women alike, don't connect this attraction with the human drive to reproduce. They only connect it with sexual attraction. God created every part of our body with a purpose in mind. We often forget that the primary purpose of physical attraction and sex is procreation and not recreation. Likewise, women are attracted to the muscles and the look of a healthier man, because this represents strong genes that will most likely produce healthy offspring. She naturally enjoys the company of a man who she feels will protect and provide for her, because this indicates what his strengths and likelihood as a good father will be. This is why, it is so important that you do not try to make your man your woman. His maleness is what defines his role in nature. He must be allowed to think as a protector, provider, and father, not as a nice, nurturing mother. His attitude toward his children should be to teach them how to survive against the adverse conditions of life, so they can reproduce more of their own kind. This is a basic God given instinct for the preservation and continuation of the species. It was God's command to Adam, "Be fruitful and multiply." This command is written into the DNA of every man.

So, when his son falls and scrapes his knee, Daddy will say, "Get up and brush it off. You're OK." It is his instinctive way of teaching his offspring to persevere, even in the event of painful setbacks. Another example of a father's life lessons would be to allow his child to experience the natural consequences of his bad decisions. He may want to allow some things to happen to his little one just for the purpose of teaching a life lesson that a mom could never stand by and just watch. In the mind of the father, he knows his child must learn how to make good decisions. When I taught my young baby child what "hot" meant, I put a cup of coffee down where I knew he could reach it and as he touched the cup I said, "Hot." After a few light touches of the cup my baby eventually said "Hot," and then point to the cup rather than touch it. From that point on if I didn't want him to touch something I would simply shout out "hot" and he wouldn't touch it. A good father would rather his child be under his watchful eye and learn these lessons early in life and be right there to help him to recover, if need be. A mom may be horrified at what she sees, because her natural instinct is to comfort and preserve, remembering she is the one who gave him life. She should never interfere or contradict these important life lessons.

Think Like a Man?

Have you ever heard the term 'scatter brain?' If you haven't, let me introduce you to the definition. It is a derogatory term used to describe a person whose mind switches from subject to subject without warning. This person finds it difficult to focus and stay on one train of thought. It is similar to Attention Deficit

Disorder (ADD). Women are sometimes thought to be scatter brain by men. This is because men process their thoughts so differently than women that it throws them off. Men are linear thinkers, for the most part. This means they typically think in a straight line. They are step-by-step logical thinkers. Too many interjections or too much interference can cause most men to feel confused and just shut down. Most men would never admit this, so you are privileged to hear this major male secret. Women and men both can multitask, but men do it the same way they think, in a straight line. A woman can think about dinner, a bill that needs to be paid, the grocery list, and her need to buy stockings when she gets gas all in the same thought while on her monthly period. Remarkable!

Women also tend to think with more details than the average man. Guys tend to think more of the big picture and the benefits. If it seems like your man doesn't hear you, it's because you are not saying the right thing for his mind. The best way to understand his brain is to visualize a group of hunters out in the wilderness trying to hunt down the prey. The way those hunters strategize is they first look at the landscape (big picture). Then they visualize the capture (benefit). They don't always consider the things in between until they see it as an obstacle to their objective. Women may see the same objective, but they see those little obstacles as major issues and may talk herself and her man out of even trying. Men are more focused on the objective and women focus on how to get there. This is why men are great hunters, they tend to use their brains and strength to deal with the obstacle as they come rather than trying to figure it all out with predictions and calculations. Men take the risk for the greater good (the benefit).

So, try to understand that you cannot force or expect a man to process his thoughts the way you do. This can be very frustrating if you think you made a simple request, but your man didn't seem to hear or understand a word you said. This will be explained in more detail in Chapter 4, *Knowing How To Talk to a Man*. The main point in this chapter is to understand that there is a major difference between men and women. It must be taken into consideration at all times and you must accept it as reality. No need to call your man stupid or think he has brain damage. He is probably just as intelligent as you are. He simply processes the information in his brain differently. Learning to appreciate this and understanding how it works in your relationship is a plus for both you and him!

TWO

Control Those Emotions

All emotions are pure which gather you and lift you up; that emotion is impure which seizes only one side of your being and so distorts you.

~Rainer Maria Rilke

Many women have been labeled as "psychos" and "crazed." It's all blamed on out of control emotions. Firstly, I think we need to differentiate between out of control emotions and bad decision making. Emotions are feelings, they are not choices. Emotions can influence decisions, but only if we allow them too. A life driven by feelings is sure to end up in shipwreck! You cannot maintain a household budget on feelings. You have to make good choices. I think many men see the emotional response of a woman's bad choice and blame the choice on the emotion. Gender has nothing to do with poor decision making. Both prisons and graveyards are filled with men and women who made bad choices. I love the following quote about feelings and choices:

Feelings are much like waves. We can't stop them from coming, but we can choose which one to surf.

~Jonathan Mårtensson

On the subject of feelings and emotions men are quick to make the word "emotions" synonymous with the word "female." It is important for a woman to know how a man's emotions work. If I gave you a set of keys you would need to know which key does what. The front door key of your house would not start the engine of your car. The car door key would not open the mail box and the list goes on. So, in like manner if you try to use the "key" that turns your emotions on or off with a man it would be like trying to use your locker room key to shut of the security alarm; it just won't work! You must try to understand how your man's emotions work without comparing them to your own.

Men are no more immune from emotions than women; we think women are more emotional, because the culture lets them give free vent to certain feelings, "feminine" ones, that is, no anger please, but it's okay to turn on the waterworks.

~Una Stannard

Most men don't even acknowledge that they have emotions, but it is because they normally associate emotions with the cycles and outburst they see some women going through. If you mention that men have cycles too, most would flatly deny you, but the truth on the matter is that scientific evidence surfaced years ago proving that men have emotional cycles as well. In 1931 a researcher by the name of Dr. Rex B. Hersey charted a man's emotions, and found that they run in cycles of crests and depressions over an average period of four to five weeks.

The emotional expression of men is just not a subject talked about in the mainstream media. Maybe it's because of the many men running the media show. Most women are completely baffled when men show emotions or the lack of them. The following is an email sent in by a website reader who is clueless about her husband's emotional state:

My husband has difficulty expressing himself in almost every area. He acts like he has a boredom issue. He was recently diagnosed with Sleep Apnea and ever since then it seems he uses it as a crutch to get out of doing anything. He takes no responsibility for nearly anything. I keep leaving the door open for the small amount of things I try and have him do. But he shows no interest in them. So how can I deal with this and try and help him. Because he also falls asleep in church, I sometimes feel like the sleep disorder is not a disorder and it is just to get out of doing the things that need to be done. He has always gotten his way all through life. Whenever he got into trouble financially or in anything someone was always there to bail him out. And now the people that he has relied on for many years have all died. And now he seems to have gone into major withdrawal and will not talk with anyone. Not even our Pastor. He really needs help. I also failed to mention that during all this about 5-6 years ago he lost his good paying job and recently we lost 15 family and friends. And during all that time there was no emotion. Not even for his adopted Mother's death. So I know something is wrong but getting to a doctor or Pastor is another whole different story.

This is a woman who can see changes going on in her husband, but cannot put her finger on the cause or a cure. She is not the first and won't be the last. It's no secret many men, and some women as well, are always joking to each other about how moody women can get and how they will never be able to fully understand the mind of a woman, but men have their own complexities when it comes down to their emotions. You don't have to be like the woman. I'm hoping after reading this book you will be better informed and have the tools that can help you have a productive relationship with your man.

I found an interesting article by Jae Ireland, in which she laid her steps to understanding the emotions of a man. I thought it was important enough to hear this "woman's" point of view on the subject and see if you make a connection that might help you better understand your man:

Overview

Men's emotions are confusing and sometimes contradict each other internally. Often, men do not even understand their own emotions. The Mayo Clinic notes that male depression often goes undiagnosed because it is difficult for men to explain what they are feeling or that they feel ashamed for not subscribing to the society "norm" of a tough, well-adjusted, providing male. Encourage your man to show his emotions by being supportive and understanding that a man's emotions are often much more complicated than he lets on.

Step 1
Realize that men often have a difficult time communicating their emotions. No man wants to tell his partner that he is sad or depressed. Instead of becoming angry that he does not want to share his emotions with you, simply let him know that you are ready when he is. Leave yourself open for that communication. Do not force the issue.

Step 2
Look for non-verbal cues to denote his emotions. Perhaps he will not tell you when he is stressed or nervous, but he always chews his nails when he is stressed about work. By watching for these cues, you can better understand how he is feeling by comparing the things he is experiencing with his physical reactions to the emotions he is feeling.

Step 3

Consider the social norms that a man is supposed to follow when it comes to emotions and sharing those emotions. Men are historically supposed to be the non-emotional providers to their partners. This does not reflect on your ability to communicate as a partner, but it will help you to understand why he is hesitant to show emotion around anyone.

Step 4

Expect emotions to be displayed as actions, rather than words. While a woman can fully articulate what she is feeling, a man is more likely to try and find a solution to the problem and work on it. In fact, when a woman constantly asks "What are you thinking?" to a man who has gone quiet, she usually assumes he's angry. He is most likely gone quiet as he thinks about how to remedy his concern.

Step 5

Give your man a platform to vent frustrations. You will see a great outpouring of emotion if you are able to disguise it as a session where he is able to vent out what he is feeling, manifested as frustration or anger. Men view frustration and anger as more masculine emotions. Even if he is feeling sad or depressed, you might find that you will see his emotion come through as a hotter emotion. (Reprinted; Found April 20, 2011 http://www.livestrong.com/article/47241-understanding-mens-emotions/#ixzz1K2VEWK25)

Doing whatever you can do to better understand how your partner processes his emotions can help to clear up misunderstandings and bring greater tolerance into your relationship. Keep at the forefront of your thinking and processing that men and women are different in more than just the obvious physical traits. Here are a few more important tips for understanding the emotions of your man.

A Quiet Man is Not Always an Angry Man

Many men have said they hate it when they are having quiet or an alone moment and their woman says to them, "So, what are you thinking about" For a woman this question is connected to their own feelings, because many women tend to get quiet or isolate when they are feeling disappointed or hurt. This is not the "key" to open the door of your man's heart especially if you want him to communicate with you.

When a man seems to be unusually quiet, it doesn't always mean that he is upset about something. In most cases it means he has a problem that he needs to solve. He may be calculating the cost or contemplating the risk of a situation that he may or may not have talked to you about. He may be trying to find the right words to say in response to something you may have asked him about prior to this quiet moment and he is playing it out in his brain first. Imagine that in his mind he has to test several phrases out before he feels he has the right phrase that will not get him chewed up and spit out. It doesn't automatically mean that he is trying to come up with a lie. There just might be an image in his mind of his woman standing there with one hand on her hip and a frying pan in the other hand waiting to see if his answer is going to be the right answer. Then he may be thinking about the bible verse that says, "A slow answer turns away wrath" and wants to calm down your wrath before he speaks.

Cool Emotions Means a Longer life for Men

Some women really wish their man was as sensitive and emotional as they are. We will read later that in most cases this just won't happen and why. They think if their man was more like them it would help them to understand them better. Not only is this the wrong way of thinking, but there are several reasons why this might not be the best overall solution for your relationship in the long run.

Dr. Rodney Pearson

Research shows that strong emotions - particularly for men - can be physically dangerous. I'm sure you have heard the term 'weaker sex' used to describe the difference between the two genders, but in some ways men might actually be the more vulnerable of the two sexes. According to the statistics women not only live longer, but at every stage of life the male is more likely to die than the female. Even in infancy, premature boys are more likely to die than premature girls. There was one study that showed that when young boys put in a room with the recorded voice of a baby crying, the boys were much quicker to try to switch off the recording of a baby crying than young girls were. The researchers at first reasoned that this was because of male insensitivity. But it turned out that the boys had much higher levels of stress hormone in their bloodstreams than the girls did on hearing the emotionally arousing trigger. The research suggests that men are actually *more sensitive* to emotion and will try to avoid it as much as possible. Your man may be shutting down his emotions as a natural life preserver. There is no way I could keep up with the ups and downs of my wife's emotions and mental processing. I must focus on one thing and that thing only and once I have that thing under control I can safely move on to the next item. Within that same time period my wife would have asked and answered the needs of several pressing issues. She amazes me!

The Action Man verses the Talking Man

Women all over are constantly saying, "He doesn't communicate with me!" I hope I can help you with this. A man's brain is not wired for communicating; it is wired for action during high emotion. Now that I've said it you probably are saying, "YES! YES! YES!" Most men act when stressed. On the other hand women's brains are wired more for talking things over. This is why most men are slow about emotions, because they may have to jump into action and the brain focus is on how to do the action and not on how to communicate it. Most men already know at what point his anger is likely to lead to an action and some of the actions might not be the best choice. So, if he doesn't slow down and consider the consequences and the ramifications of his action he may not think that one bad action or reaction might affect his entire generation and generations thereafter.

Remember women, you want your man to keep a cool head. Let him think things through as long as he needs to, especially if the final decision about something major is resting on his shoulders. Don't forget, you may need him to help calm you down when you have just launched into a rampage that you can't seem to pull back out of.

Fight or Flight

When a man finds himself in a highly emotionally charged situation, his first thought is normal: fight back or to leave the situation. Like with most animals a man instinctively would rather avoid a dangerous situation. If he can walk away without looking weak it will be his first choice, but to protect pride or property he will fight. This is how a man is internally constructed. He can sense that things are going to get ugly and the more he is pushed the more difficult it is for him to walk away. If he doesn't remove himself quick enough he may become very emotional. The body begins to send out signals and this may cause his blood pressure to skyrocket and he is at risk of having a heart attack. It also takes much longer for a man's blood pressure and immune system to return to normal after high emotion than it does for a woman. But a man may gain control of himself quicker than a woman can. So often when your man senses all of these things happening in him, he will instinctively try to protect himself and escape the situation. But will the woman let him? This is where domestic violence gets its high numbers from. In many cases (not all) the man is trying to get back control to walk away, but the woman continues to push him. She lashes out with insults. She may even become physical, not always to protect herself but to hurt him. I have heard of some women who actually block the door with their bodies to stop a man who is trying to leave a dangerous situation before someone gets hurt.

If the above situation sounds like something you would do, let me advise you that you should never try to force your man to do anything. In many of those situations where you try to get physical someone is likely to get hurt. It's best to get control of your emotions and step away from the situation. The chances of things escalating are very likely.

Let's Get an Understanding

Please listen when I say that most men don't understand or know that women need to vent. They don't like it and have a hard time staying put when you are venting. They want to fix the situation, and, therefore, the only dialogue they want to engage in is that which pertains to fixing the problem. Women, you need to know that most men may prefer to talk about practicalities and logic rather than how he, or you for that matter, is feeling about anything.

This is why when your man sees that you are upset or stressed out about something, he will ask you if you want to talk about it and then offer advice or tell you what he thinks you should or should not do. Most men don't connect with just listening to you and affirming your feelings when you need to just vent as part of the fixing process, and most women don't know how to tell him that without first getting upset over the fact that he's trying to fix it.

The bottom line is this, asking your man, "How do you feel?" may not get you the straight answer you expect and be careful if you're about to say, "I feel." The word "feel" just doesn't do well with most men unless it's after we eat or during sex and they will usually answer, "I feel good" or "Can I have more?!" If it wasn't good, most men would just say nothing.

Men would rather you help them come up with a solution rather than talk about feelings, but you have to be careful with that as well. You may want to try to say something like, "What do you think about doing such-and-such about that?" A man can see this as part of his problem solving process. Also women, don't try to help your man by criticizing him on past decisions that may have been wrong. IT NEVER WORKS! If you think telling a man what he should have done will help him, let me tell you that it is another one of those wrong keys we mentioned earlier.

Now these last words in this chapter may be the most difficult words for you to hear or do. There will be times when your man will mess something up so bad and you feel like you must tell him exactly how you feel. You feel that venting is the only thing you can do and if you don't you are going to bust! Resist the temptation of feeling that you always have to say what you think. Sometimes not saying anything is a much better strategy than spewing your anger or rubbing in the fact that you were right. Silence can be your best friend if you know when to speak and when not to speak. Let me close this chapter with three quotes that might save your marriage:

Silence is the secret to sanity.

~Astrid Alauda

Silence is one of the hardest arguments to refute.

~Josh Billings

There are times when silence has the loudest voice.

~Leroy Brownlow

Control Your Emotions!

THREE

Keep It Simple Sister (K.I.S.S)

Let's start this chapter by reading another friendly email from a woman who doesn't understand how to keep it simple for her man:

I can become irritated when I am sad and hurt, and my boyfriend walks away from me during those times that I need his support most. I am going through a hard life event and whenever there is negative progress in the event that makes me sad, he walks away. Two days ago I had one of those bad days, and when I saw him I was impatient and already very sad with my own event. He annoyed me over something simple and I told him that I wanted to be alone. Although he saw me in deep pain he walked away and did not even call the next day to check to see if I was alright. I am talking about a major event, not trivial. Although I am emotional, I don't sweat the small stuff. When I told him how much I was hurt with him not supporting and caring for me he said I wanted to be alone. Are we women different or is it only him like this that when our loved one is in deep pain, for once we can put ourselves at the back? Would you leave your woman alone even though she told you she wants to be alone, when you see her in deep pain?

This boyfriend probably thought to himself, "If I don't know what to say, it's better to say nothing at all." How simple can you get? She said, "Leave me alone," and then got mad because her boyfriend did what she asked him to do. This is why men get so confused with women. I mentioned before most men think in a straight line. It's called linear thinking. Rarely do their thoughts bounce around in their heads or take detours like the thought of many women. It's not unusual for a man to say, "We'll solve that problem when we get there." This is because in his process of solving the problem he deals with the issues one step at a time. That is how he watches TV, reads the paper or even pursues sex!

For example, my son-in-law and I took the girls out for dinner and a movie. The girls were my wife and our daughter. He and I watched the movie intensely, enjoying every moment. The girls asked questions and made assumptions throughout the whole movie. Every few minutes, one of them would blurt out, "Why is she doing that? Where is she going? Do you think he did it?" and so on and so on. I always say to my wife when these questions come up, "I don't know, but if you just watch the movie we'll both find out." Once the process begins men don't like to be distracted. It will all be clear eventually. This is why men don't like to be disturbed when they are watching sports. They are watching the process of the competition. We don't want to just know who won. If we have a choice, we want to see the process rather than try to figure it out.

One of the most confusing things for men is trying to figure out the difference between what a woman is saying verses what she means. I believe that this is something that men have had difficulty with for thousands of years! Women ask how do I look, but often they don't want to hear what you really think. Learning how to keep it simple is being aware that sending mixed messages is never *simple*. You need to be as clear as possible as to what you want and what you don't want.

Also be aware because in this linear style of thinking and processing there is a start point and a finishing that most men try to stick to. With that in mind you should not try to start something that you can't commit to finishing. This actually gets a lot of guys in trouble, because many women change their minds right in the middle of the process. It's okay for a woman to do that if she's out shopping or hanging out with other girls, but changing your mind mid-stream is problematic for most men and it can put a major strain on a relationship.

An extreme example of this is many guys who are convicted of "date rape" say, "She led me on!" This is no excuse and it rarely holds as a defense in court. However, as unfortunate as it is, there are times when a man is able to prove that the women made him feel that the sex was what she wanted just as much as he did. When a man won his case, it was usually because the women failed to prove that she was clear about the change in her intentions. You may ask, "How can that be?" In an article entitled *Acquaintance Rape Date Rape* the author reviews the results of a study that addresses, "Why Nice Men Force Sex on Their Friends?"

Some men feel that a particular female behavior permits a man to force a woman to have sex. Charlene L. Mulenhard of Texas A&M University and Richard McFall of Indiana University reported the results of a study in which 106 college students were asked to respond anonymously about acceptable behavior in dating situations. The subjects were given descriptions of three types of dates that varied in respect to who initiated the date, where the couple went, and who paid. They were then asked if there were any circumstances in which forced sex was justified. Men rated intercourse against the woman's wishes as significantly more justifiable when the woman initiated the date, when the man paid and when the couple went to the man's apartment. UCLA researchers posed similar questions to teens. A high percentage of the male teens felt that forced sex was acceptable if the woman said yes and then changed her mind (54%), if he spent a lot of money on her (39%), if she "led him on" (54%), and if he is so turned on that he thinks he can't stop (36%).

You still may feel that this is totally unjustifiable and it may be, but remember the purpose of this book is to help you understand how a man thinks. Here's another story to help see the "simplified" male point of view.

A couple looked at a brochure and they decided to take a trip to the top of the summit together for a date. The woman volunteered to drive and picked him up in her car. They were glad to be together and have looked forward to this date for a long time. They walked up from the parking lot laughing and enjoying each other. He paid the park entry fee and from there they had to hike up the mountain to reach the first level of the summit trip. In the man's mind they were both going down the same path together hand-in-hand when suddenly the one path split and became two narrow parallel paths, one path for him and the other for her. The paths were side by side, but they were talking and having so much fun that he never noticed when the split took place.

Then, they got into specially designed vehicles to take them the rest of the way of the trip. He wasn't alarmed because they were both still headed in the same direction and seemed to be headed to the same eventual destination only now the designs of the two paths were very different. His path was a straight line with no stops, guaranteeing a quick arrival to the top of the summit. Her path was a very different scenic route with hilly curves, sightseeing points of interest, rest stops and refueling stations for the vehicles along the way. He got to the end destination a bit before and didn't see her, so he paid for reservations for them both to go to the next level of their trip which is the summit, but his traveling companion was still making stops and viewing the sights. He jumped into another vehicle and hurried back down his path to find a way to reach her and he saw that she had run out of gas. He tried to get her to get on board with him, but now she was caught up with the beautiful scenery, and said she didn't want to go to the summit at all. She felt comfortable and wanted to stay here for now. He had paid for this trip that she agreed to and helped to plan. Reservations were made, time was spent getting to this point and he was not turning back now. Since he was a problem solver by nature, in a last ditch effort of desperation to "fix" this he tried harder to convince her to come with him, but she still kindly refused him.

He became angry and confused with her abrupt change and thought, "I know that this is what you really want to do, but you're just distracted by the scenery or maybe you're a little afraid of heights. I know once you get there you'll be glad you did just like you did with the sushi I convinced you to try last week. You didn't want to try it at first and now you love it!" So he pushed her in his vehicle and took her to the top of the summit. When they reaches the peak of the summit he let out a huge exhale of relief and was now completely satisfied that he came and also glad he made her come. He looked over toward his date and to his surprise she had did not come up the top of the summit with him. Moments before arriving at the peak she had jumped out of the vehicle. He was so taken by the summit peak that he never noticed that was she no longer with him. She had jumped out of the moving vehicle and was cut and bruised all over. She was hurting and not happy at all. When he came down off of the mountaintop he saw her there crying and bleeding. He asked her, "What happened to you, I thought you were coming to the summit with me?" She said I tried to tell you I didn't want to go, but you tried to force me any way. His response was, "Well, at first you said you wanted to go. You were excited and you got me all excited. I bought the tickets and then you changed your mind when we were almost there. I thought you were just a little afraid. I thought it was like the sushi. I didn't think you were really serious. Sorry…but it really was beautiful up there. You want to do it again?"

This is the common, simple mindset of most men compared to the mindset of the average woman. A man's mind flows in the simplest and straightest path possible. Women take in the sights, highs and lows and most anything else along the way. Most men will gravitate towards that which is the simplest. Most of the men you know don't like shopping like you do or more specifically they do like shopping the way you shop. A typical man goes shopping for a specific item or items he is looking to purchase. He doesn't find joy in just looking at things unless he knows that he needs it. Women go shopping and do just that…shop! You may hit every store you like and shop with nothing specific in your mind. If you do have something particular you are looking for, it could take a while to settle on that thing even if it is what you are looking for, because you think, "I might find something better."

Some women check out different sales just because there is a sale with no real consideration for anything except for the fact that you can get it much cheaper if you buy it now even if you have no plans on using it any time soon! The typical man would never do that even if he can save money. If he can't use it, he won't buy it for later. This doesn't mean that women are better shoppers. I am a much more efficient grocery shopper than my wife when it comes down to getting the most with the budget we have to work with. My wife gets more variety and experiments with different tastes and colors. We are very different shoppers.

Let's deal for a moment about how a woman might connect with a man. Many women tend to think that when a man approaches them their female intuition will allow them to quickly map out his intentions and motivation during the initial conversation. There may be some times when this is true, but then again at other times it is absolutely not. Many times a woman can have one conversation and tell if a man is secure, insecure, needy, prideful, difficult, complex, a romantic, a fighter, a street thug, a high risk taker, or the absolute gentleman just in their initial meeting. This has been proven over and over again. However, some men are master manipulators as I have written in my book *Exposing Manipulation*. They may be simple, but are not always simple minded and they know how to play the game and reading a woman's responses and reactions is what they do well. A manipulating man will become the man that they know you desire or need for them to be at your moment of vulnerability. So don't take a man's simple desire, simple pleasure or simple lifestyle for granted.

My advice is as simple as the subject, just *Keep It Simple Sister!* Be aware that keeping it simple for him may be very difficult for you. You may have to save the details for later. You can't always include all the colors, fragrances and other cute nuances that many women so easily pick up when describing or painting a mental picture for him to see. So try not to get too mad when he abruptly stops you in the middle of your sharing a thought and says, "So what's the point?" He doesn't value those details in the same way that you do. He only wants to hear the details that will affect him. When that happens, just stop for a moment and try to focus on the main point. That is all your man wants to hear, and all he will mentally process unless you're describing a super monster dunk in a basketball game or some new electronic gadget! For example: A woman might say, " I was on my way home from getting my hair done and I was running late to pick up the kids and this car ran the red light and hit me! Can you come and get me? I didn't get hurt but I can't believe how he ran through the red light!" If you were telling this same thing to a man, all he wants to hear is. "Honey, I just had a car accident. I'm ok can you come get me?"

Good communication is very important if you want to have a productive and healthy relationship with your man. Next you will read a great chapter that will tell you all about "Man Talk." It goes further into how a man hears and speaks and is one of the most important chapters in this book. Read it like it's your bible!

Study it and practice what you learn, but always remember when you talk to a man, (Keep it seriously simple (K.I.S.S.) for your man as much as possible! You will both be glad that you did!

FOUR

Know How To "Talk Man"

"Talking Man" is a skill that every woman should acquire some level of competence. I remember watching a movie version of the classic comic book Richie Rich. In the movie the little rich kid wanted to play baseball with a group of junior sluggers who had a game going on in a neighborhood sandlot. All the kids seemed to be good at the game and were really enjoying themselves, but there seemed to be something different about one of the boys. This boy seemed to be smaller, but a bit better than the rest of the boys. The little boy screamed out, "Come hit the ball!" The other kids all laughed and agreed. As it turned out, this little boy was actually a little girl and the only girl in the group. The character was the tom-boy that most young male gangs have at least one of. She was athletic, well respected and in most cases thought of as "one of the guys." Eventually age got the best of them and the young boyish girl started to show signs of femininity that started to conflict with the relationships. The one thing that made or broke the camaraderie was their communication. What got the girl on the inside with the guys was how well she "talked man." The little girl was not as big as the guys, but she talked as big. She showed her bravery with fearlessness in her voice, even if her counterparts were shaking in their little boots.

The key to "Talking Man" is not talking like a man or sounding like a man, but knowing what men listen to. Typically men don't listen to the paragraph long sentences that many women use to convey a simple thought. The fact is that most women rarely have simple thoughts. Women usually have complex pieces to their thoughts on any given issue. They tend to ask more questions and need more information than many men, because they are processing more than one angle of that thought. Men tend to see the big picture and visualize the outcome more than the process. Women often can't see the big picture until they work out all the other issues of the process in their minds. So, when a woman explains herself it can be like a mental journey and she assumes the man is following her thought pattern and in most cases she finds herself alone for most of the trip. Most men tend to shut the voice of the woman out after they think they got the main point. Women have a tendency to share not only your main points but how you felt or currently feel about those points, not even realizing that your man probably stopped listening after your first sentence.

When men hear a woman talking, they usually first determine how important is what they are hearing to their life. The level of importance will be analyzed in that first sentence or two. Have you noticed how many times you may ask your man, "Are you listening to me?" and his answer is "yes." He is listening, but somewhere in the conversation he has determined that what you were saying had a low level of importance relative to other things he may be considering at the time. I DIDN'T SAY, NO IMPORTANCE! Remember the key phrase here is "low levels of importance," which is very different than, no importance at all.

Read to the following sentence. Which part of sentence do you think the husband heard?:

"Honey, I'm going to the beauty salon to get my hair done. Then I'm going to drop the kids off at the church for choir practice. Can you take the turkey out of the oven in about an hour? Oh and the clothes will be ready to be picked up at the cleaners at two o'clock today, if you have time can you go pick them up? I'll fix dinner when I get back home...okay?" He replies, "Okay, Honey have fun!" Chances are, the only thing he heard was, "Honey, I'm going..." and "I'll fix dinner when I get back home...okay?"

An inexperienced wife might come home mad and fussing with her husband. She probably will accuse him of neglecting the house, being inconsiderate of all the work she does and tell him to make his own dinner. An experienced wife might call in about an hour after she leaves and simply say, "How does the turkey look, Honey?" Her husband would probably say, "Oh the turkey looks good!" Then get up and go take the turkey out the oven and see the reminder note she left on the stove that says, "Don't forget to pick up the clothes from the cleaners! Thanks for all your help, Honey! See ya for dinner!" The first woman would probably have a short and tense relationship. The second woman learned the art of "Talking Man" and would have a good chance of a long and fulfilling relationship.

The little girl in the Richie Rich movie didn't have to fight about getting in with the guys; she probably just hooked into their interest which was baseball. There are always women who seem to get along with guys better than other women and it is often because they talk about what is interesting to him. I know that someone is reading this and saying, "What about my interests?" Well, let me remind you that this book is about you pleasing him (I do address a lot about good communication in my book *20 ½ Ways for a Man to Love His Woman*). I will say that if you learn how to make your interests interesting to him, you'll get his attention.

"Talking Man" means to get to the point! Certain men may not need all the details you need. They usually could care less about the smell, the color, the way the small flower thing was put on the big shining thing or how so and so is going to hate or love it when they get it. Most men just want to know if they have to do anything with it and if so when, where and how long will it take?

When you are talking to a man, remember it is not that he doesn't care, but rather he is concerned with what will or can he do with the information. The color doesn't matter to him unless he can do something with knowing the color. When you ask the average man, "Isn't that pretty?" it is a meaningless question unless he can assign the word "pretty" to something of meaning for him. Think about it for a moment. What is pretty? For a woman something that is pretty will create a pleasant emotion when they see it. For most men something that is pretty is feminine. I can remember going shopping with my wife for a piece of furniture. While she was demonstratively waving her arms with her eyes bright with excitement telling me how pretty it is, my only concern was why do you want it, what will we do with it and even more important, if it will fit.

There are many important things to remember in "Talking Man." The point is that you want to communicate in the most effective way possible at all times. Here are a few things to remember in your conversations with the man in your life:

1. Men are mostly linear thinkers. For the most part they thi nk in a straight line. Don't jump from topic to subtopic in a current conversation. Most men don't care about anythi ng other than the main point. Men cannot bounce around

from one subject to the next as many women can do. Thi s means if you want a man to follow your train of thought, you cannot talk as you feel.

2. Remember get to the point as quickly as possible. It woul d do you good to make the main point first. Add the expl anation later.

3. Only add the details if they are important to the main poi nt. Here's an example: "Honey, the shop is at 555 W. Mai n Street. It's next door to that cute little coffee shop we w ent to one time with the green curtains I loved!" Why bri ng up the coffee shop at all unless you went there enough for him to connect it to the shop you are talking about. H e probably doesn't remember the coffee shop or the curta ins.

4. No hints! Tell your man exactly what you want. Hinting o nly complicates things. If you want him to try to figure ou t what you are thinking or you want him to fill in the blan ks, you are more than likely to be very disappointed. The biggest complaints that men have is, "My wife wants me t o be a mind reader!" It is torture for a man to try to figure out what his woman wants. Often the woman doesn't kn ow what she wants and is using her man to help her sort t hrough her emotions. It drives him crazy!

5. Don't try to figure out what your man is going to say befo re he says it. He may seem to be predictable, but let him s ay what he is thinking or what he may feel about a certain thing. Sometimes he just may fool you with a response th

at you weren't expecting.

6.   Men don't feel your emotions, but they hear them. When you get upset about an issue your man is usually not feelin g what you feel. They hear your complaint, but they don't feel it with you. They hear your excitement, but they don' t feel it with you. They hear your expressions, but in most cases they don't feel that same emotion that you feel.

7.   Never cross your points. If you make the point that you n eed him to go to the store, don't cross it with your disapp ointment about him not going yesterday. Your cross poin t statement might come out like this: "Honey, I asked you to go to the store yesterday and you didn't go. What do I need to do for you to go to the store for me today? Are y ou going to wait until the kids starve to death first?"

8.   Timing of a conversation is as important as the conversat ion itself. Remember men are linear thinkers, so why do y ou want to discuss an important topic while he is watchin g TV. Some women assume that if the TV show, video ga me or whatever her man is doing is not important to her, it should not be important to her man. Don't discuss his l ack of employment when you clearly see he wants to be s exually intimate. Wait for the right time. Especially if it's a complaint.

9.   Compliments can go a long way. Many times the best way to discuss a sensitive issue is to start with a compliment ra ther than a complaint. For instance, if you want your man to take out the trash and he never seems to have time, try

this one day: "Honey, I was thinking about how much I e njoyed going to the movies last week with you. I love spe nding time with you alone. Would you like to walk aroun d the block together? Good, can you take out that stinky t rash right quick and I'll get our shoes? Thanks, sweetheart!"

10. Never bait and switch! This means you get him hooked to do a small thing, but then you switch it to a big thing. Let me give you some examples of that. Don't tell your husba nd you want him to go to the store to get a couple of thin gs then hand him a four page grocery list. Never say, "Let 's stop by my mother's house," but the stop by turns into lunch, dinner and a scrap book session. Never say can yo u give me a minute, but it turns into an hour. Your man w ill never trust your word and you will have problems getti ng him to do anything.

These are just a few of the things that go wrong when women are trying to communicate with their man. I'm sure the list could go on and on, but if you start practicing your daily "Talking Man" skills you will find that it is easier and becomes more a part of your communication as time goes on! Good communication between a man and a woman is an essential part of building a healthy relationship. Trust me when I say this, it is much easier for you to learn how to "Talk Man" than it is for him to learn how to "Talk Woman."

FIVE

Let Him Fix It (especially if it isn't broken)

Men find their self-esteem in their worth. You can make any man your friend by making him feel that he has worth to you. You may say that women need compliments and sympathy too and you would be right, but understand that it doesn't drive you or your dear sisters the way it does a man. Letting a man know that he is needed taps directly into how he feels about himself. You may never know this, but many men internally fight all day for his self-worth and dominance or at least some level of respect in the workplace but he doesn't want to feel as if he has to work for it at home. Your man wants to come home and feel that he is the king of the castle and you are his willing submissive queen ready to serve him.

You probably don't mind being the queen, but the only problem with that is that you want some loyal subjects who are ready to serve you too! After all, what queen has to wash her own dishes? Often in today's society where gender roles are not as defined as they used to be, women feel that they are just as entitled to having their needs met and those needs may be a foot massage after a long day in one or two inch pumps, a roasted chicken, some chocolate ice cream and a bubble bath. If you could have it your way, having sex might be a few items down on the "to do" list that night after being pampered and petted in a clean house. This might be your idea of the perfect way to end that particular day. Most men never understand, believe or accept that sometimes a woman just wants to relax without sex being on the agenda occasionally. Trust me ladies, it's just not part of our biological make up until somewhere after 50 years old.

As a wife you must find a balance of making your man feel as though he is the best thing since sliced salami on toasted bread and getting your own needs met. One of the best ways of doing that is to build up your man's self-esteem. He needs it and usually wants it from you, more than anyone else! The best wife a man can have is one who knows how to make him feel good, with or without sex.

A man needs to know that he can fix something, even if it's not broken. I know you're thinking, "That's ridiculous!" It's all about his self worth. He needs to know that you need him for something other than making the house payments or mowing the lawn. It makes him feel good when he knows that you see him as a necessary part of your life. Don't judge him based on what he does or doesn't do or hasn't accomplished yet. Learn the benefits of complimenting him for the small things you may take for granted. Does he come home to you every night? Does he take time to love and discipline the children? Can you call on him if the car breaks down and at a minimum he'll come pick up and get you safely home? Do you feel protected in your home because he's there?

He needs to know that you appreciate even these small things verses always finding an opportunity to complain about something he hasn't done. He's going to make mistakes, but make the good things that he does stand out more than the bad things that you may have difficulty letting go.

Here's a story you may appreciate that makes my point. Amber was a loving wife who did everything she could to make her home a place of love and peace. Her husband Max was the kind of guy who didn't like doing yard work at all and they had an extra-large corner lot and the ground had fertile, perfect conditions for grass to grow. One day she walked in and saw that the grass had grown up in the backyard and it was time to get it cut. She knew that although Max always did a good job mowing the lawn, he hated doing it and avoided it like it was the plague. Amber was in a bind, because tomorrow her family was coming over for their annual 4th of July family picnic…in the backyard!

Max was pretty stressed out and tired from working overtime every day for two weeks straight. She thought hard about how she could get Max to do the yard without causing a big argument. Knowing how kind hearted Max was she said to him, "Baby, can you teach me how to cut the lawn as well as you do it?" Max had never gotten a compliment for doing the lawn. He saw it as a terrible hot job that no one could do but him. He looked at Amber and said "It's nothing good about it you just start up the lawn mower and push." Being a quick thinker Amber said, "Baby, I have seen some yards that I would be ashamed of after they have been cut. You make the lawn look like freshly cleaned carpet and I'm always so proud to live in this home. I know you hate it, but I think you're the best and you do it just for me! So teach me how you do it!" Max went straight to the garage, got the lawn mower and mowed with a big quarter moon smile on his face as his wife watched and cheered him on with a periodic ice cold soda and a big kiss after he was done. She helped with getting rid of the cut grass and they laughed and talked through the whole job. Max never saw the harsh job of cutting the lawn as he had seen it before. It became a partnership between him and his dear wife. Amber used wisdom and kindness rather than demanding that Max get his lazy butt up and get the lawn mowed before the family arrived, so she would not be so embarrassed!

Letting him fix it means that you may have to back off of doing things you could do yourself sometimes, but, just like Amber in our example, you must use wisdom. Amber saw that her husband was actually a good guy, but he didn't value a nice looking lawn, at least not enough to keep it nice himself. She used wisdom by using that which he did value to get the lawn done. Max did value what his wife thought of him, so she used that in a positive way.

Now, I know some of you might say that Max should love his own yard enough to want to keep it nice looking and maybe you're right. He should, but he didn't. You can't get stuck on what you think your man should do or should want to do. You must deal with where he is and not where you want him to be. Too many women want to change their man, then they get discouraged when his ways stay the same. There was a comedian by the name of Flip Wilson who used to say, "What you see is what you get, baby!" This applies to your man. You must love him where he is and for what he is.

If you're considering marriage, don't marry for a person's potential, because what you see as potential may not be what he sees as potential. If he can't see it, it won't happen. Marry the man you see in front of you. If you see a stagnated boring person, that is what you are getting. If you see someone pushing to do something with his life, then that is what you'll get. If you see a person with no spiritual values, then that is what you'll get. If he is not affectionate, don't expect affection from him. Too many women get desperate and don't want to stay single, so they marry just to avoid being alone. Then they end up being alone anyway, because the marriage doesn't last or they become their husband's roommate.

Letting him fix it also means not pushing him away when he is trying to fix you. Now I know this may irritate you at times, but this must change if you're doing it. That would be like a man pushing you away when you want to show him affection. Fixing is in his nature. It is how he shows you that he cares. It's his way of taking care of you and protecting you. He may not know how to respond to your needs any other way. I often hear people say, "Men, stop trying to fix your wife." Well, he is going to fix something, because it is what makes him feel needed. So I say to you, understand how to accept your husband's "fixing it." It is his love language. It is his way of being your overseer and protecting you. If you can interpret his fixing in a different way, it may help you not to feel belittled or degraded as so many women do. They say things like, "He makes me feel like a child" or "He acts like I can't think for myself." Turn those thoughts around in your mind. Try to reinterpret his attempt to "fix it" as a gentle kiss or a nice back rub from him, instead of a jab in your rib cage.

Many times women with low self-esteem and very independent women struggle the most with this. They interpret the "fix it" as meaning "there is something wrong with me." This is a bad message being played in their heads. If this applies to you, maybe you were told some hurtful things growing up and that recording keeps playing back in your mind and anything perceived by you as help becomes offensive. This very thought has made the bed for many divorcees and many couples had to sleep in it all alone.

SIX

See What He Sees

You may hate me by now, but I promise you that your husband, boyfriend or future knight in shining armor would love me, if he knew what I'm writing right now! Women come in all shapes, sizes, colors and other descriptions. Some women have long hair and some have short hair. Some are in the house of good health and other are on the porch of death. Where ever or whatever you are in life, you must be real about what you see in the mirror. Your man may see you totally different than how you see yourself.

Many women see themselves in comparison to someone else. This wouldn't be so bad, if it were not for the distorted view that society has on women. Someone may think they must look like a professional runway model to be attractive. While others are living a lie covering up everything. Let me tell you about my good friend Trina.

Trina was a nice young lady with a great personality, beautiful smile and sparkling glowing eyes. She had one problem, she was about 100 overweight. Everyone loved Trina including the guys at her job. Her greatest gift seemed to be in how well she dressed and kept her hair up. So it wasn't unusual for her to have men flirting with her or other women jealous of her. Her overweight body had one advantage and that was a nice bouncy breast size. So from the carnal eyes of most men she looked great! On the other hand her marriage wasn't doing great at all. Her husband told her that he was not attracted to her any longer and was having trouble getting an erection for sexual intercourse. Trina believed that the real problem had to be that there was another woman in his life because many other men were attracted to her all the time. Once they had an argument and Trina mentioned to her husband that Davis, her coworker, gave her compliments almost every day. Her husband responded to her in a fit of anger, "They flirt with you, because they see you all dressed up. But I see you naked and without your make up." This was a place of much contention for the couple and they did eventually break up.

Trina could not and would not see herself as her husband saw her. She saw herself as she wanted others to see her. Trina is not all to blame for her flaw. Our society celebrates what it determines as "beauty" over any other attribute a female may have. One of the first things a woman learns as a girl is that her appearance is very important. Parents spend hours on their little girl to make them pretty. Everyone gawks at her and makes a fuss over her if she really happens to be the "cute" one in a group of average kids. She always gets picked first or at least never last. Pageants are organized to compete for the most beautiful girl. Other formal and informal contests focus on the strength of a girl's good looks over everything else. One well known R&B singer by the name of Dr. Hook sings the song "When You're In Love with a Beautiful Woman." Some of the first words of the song speak the sentiments of our western culture,

"When you're in love with a beautiful woman, it's hard
Everybody wants her, everybody loves her
Everybody wants to take your baby home"

With this mindset in place as a standard, why would a girl or woman want to see herself as anything other than beautiful? Most pretty girls in our culture want to be prettier. Average looking girls fantasize of being the most popular girls in the school. Girls who feel that they are unattractive battle with depression and often have difficulty socializing.

There is nothing wrong with wanting to be beautiful, but it is better to want to be the best looking woman that you can be and you must be honest with yourself about your looks to do that. Don't fool yourself into thinking that you're man should love you no matter how you look. Men are designed by God to be attracted to certain specifics of a woman's appearance but attraction only attracts…it doesn't keep your man with you. There will always be someone more beautiful than you, but if you look the best that you can look and be the best that you can be you will draw the right person your way and keep him.

Now don't misunderstand what I just wrote. If you are 50 pounds overweight and say to yourself, "This is the best that I can do" you may be wrong and in denial. If you're overweight because of a medical illness or some physiological limitation then you may be doing the best that you can do. If your nose is disproportionately large for your face and you don't have the money to fix it then you may be doing the best that you can do. Can you be beautiful and overweight? The answer is yes and there are some men who are more attracted to larger women that to smaller women but that should not be your reason for overeating. The lack of discipline or even inconvenience is no excuse for you not being the best woman you can be for your man but even more so for yourself!

Listen lady, the point of this chapter is to say you can't keep the truth under all the makeup and girdles under all the work you put into keeping it covered. I'm simply saying that you're only fooling yourself if you think he hasn't noticed that your appearance has changed over the years. Yes, it is true that as he grows older he focuses less on appearance but that doesn't mean he will ignore it completely.

So your question might be, "So what should I do?"

Here are a few things to just keep in mind that your man wants me to tell you:

1. Stress eating can destroy your good looks. Learn to use other things to cope with your stress rather than ice cream or chicken and waffles. Go window shopping (without the credit card) or see a movie (without the bucket of popcorn). Maybe exercising or picking up an artsy hobby might work for you. If you're a stress eater you may need some outside help or intervention but you must be honest. Stress eating is common because we are looking for something that makes us feel better but actually may cause you to feel worse about yourself over time.

2. Combine good looks and comfort. Looking good for your man is important but you don't have to always look like you're attending a royal wedding when you're at home. Find that balance of neat casual beauty and informal comfort. You don't have to try to look sexy when you're cleaning the house but you don't want to look like a homeless hobo either. There may be times when you have to sacrifice appearance to get a job done but that should be the exception and not the norm, like every day when you get home from work. I knew a woman who when her husband asked her why she l

ooked so different when she's at home with him she s aid, "When I'm at home I'm not trying to impress no body." It was clear that she didn't think her husband was worth impressing.

3. Be real about your baseline. If you wear a wig or weav e, have fake eyelashes, lipstick, blush, support bra, gir dle, facial makeup including mascara, eyeliner and eye shadow, painted or fake finger nails, high heel shoes, s tockings, and a panty girdle; where is the real you? Yo ur husband may not even recognize you when you co me to bed. Baseline is your starting point. If your man only knows the "made up" you and the "made up" yo u is so far from baseline that you avoid her; then there is something very wrong. This could be a sign of serio us self-esteem issues that may need to be addressed w ith some professional intervention. Set your standard closer to baseline. Sometimes less is better. Enhance y our beauty, don't masquerade it with a fake make over.

Don't make excuses for your own faults. Nobody is perfect and it's so much better to be real with your faults. Some people really have problems with admitting when they make mistakes. Your man can see your faults just as good as you can see his. I had a friend who just couldn't handle her spouse pointing out her mistakes. She would be so angry over him bringing up the mistake and she would never admit or deal with her error.

SEVEN

Make Your Man Feel Important

Earlier I mentioned the prostitute. She may be hated by women with her sinful ways; luring men of every creed and color into her adulteress bed of shameless debauchery. Say or think what you will, but if men didn't have a need for what she offers, she wouldn't have any customers.

I read a very interesting article entitled "*Why Men Do Stupid Things: The Psychological Appeal of Prostitutes*" by Michael Bader a psychologist and psychoanalyst in San Francisco. Michael writes, "*Having studied the dynamics of sexual arousal for almost 15 years, and having treated dozens of men who find prostitutes irresistible, I have found that for the overwhelming majority of them, the appeal lies in the fact that, after payment is made, <u>the woman is experienced as completely devoted to the man -- to his pleasure, his satisfaction, his care, his happiness.</u> The man doesn't have to please a prostitute, doesn't have to make her happy, doesn't have to worry about her emotional needs or demands. He can give or take without the burden of reciprocity. He can be entirely selfish. He can be especially aggressive or especially passive, and not only is the woman not upset,*

she acts aroused. He is not responsible for her in any way. <u>She is entirely</u>
<u>focused on him. He is the center of the world.</u> Now, of course, these
interactions are scripted. The prostitute is acting. But it doesn't matter. For
men who like to go to prostitutes, the illusion of authenticity is enough.

I used this piece of the article, not to tell you that, as a woman, you should model you wifely duties after a prostitute, but rather to say, "These girls are on to something!" Pay attention to the principle. Every woman wants her man to make her feel that she is the center of his world; and that, that is a fair and warranted desire. But most women feel that her man already is the center of her world; otherwise she would not cook, clean, have his babies, or carry out most of these expected routines; and then be ready for sexual ecstasy for the 2.7 minutes it may take her husband to reach a climax. Afterwards, he rolls over and snores at maximum levels, while she stares at the ceiling in the dark. The prostitute will make herself available so that the man can eventually find himself at that same place of "maximum snore." She has concluded that this is what she is there to do. The "maximum snore" is a physical sign of total relaxation and satisfaction. He's not solving problems, fixing the broken blinds or negotiating which bills to pay. He wants to be released momentarily from the responsibility of "carrying the load." He wants to feel that time of sexual pleasure that is directed at him, and in his mind, is his well-deserved reward. Men need this so bad that some will pay to get it from a completely unknown stranger.

When you as a woman see this as a core need of your man, as the paid prostitutes do, your response to his need may change. Now, before you shout out, WHAT ABOUT MY NEEDS" (you probably already said it) remember, this is not a book about your needs. Buy my book *20 ½ Ways for a Man to Please His Woman* and give it to your man for that. This book is to help you keep your man happy! I promise you that most men would rather have that come from his loving and caring wife than a faceless whore. Most men will serve their wife and family with diligence, but he needs his wife to refill his tank of emotional fuel and his feeling important is the best brand of that fuel he can get! Admittedly he might not have a clue as to what your needs are but let it not said that you didn't what his needs were.

Read these powerful lyrics that were sung by R&B superstar and singing legend Gladys Knight. The song is entitled,

"If I Were Your Woman"

If I were your woman And you were my man
You'd have no other woman, You'd be weak as a lamb
If you had the strength, To walk out that door
My love would overrule my sense, And I'd call you back for more.

If you were my woman, and you were my man

She tears you down Darling, Says you're nothing at all
But I'll pick you up Darling, When she lets you fall
You're like a diamond, And she treats you like glass
Yet you make it hard to love you, But Baby don't ask

If I were your woman, Here's what I'd do
I'd never no, no, no stop loving you

Yeah, Life is so crazy, And love is unkind
Because she came first, Will she hang on your mind
You're a part of me, And you don't even know it
I'm what you need, But I'm too afraid to show it

If I were your woman, here's what I'd do
I'd never, no, no, no stop loving you

Dr. Rodney Pearson

If I were your woman
Here's what I'd do
I'd never, never, never stop loving you
If I were your woman
You're sweet lovin' woman

If I were your woman...you'd need no other woman

This is a song that in between the struggles of life and the unexpected hardships, every man wants to hear his wife sing these words with her actions.

Here are more lyrics to another song!

"You're The Best Thing That Ever Happened to me"

I've had my share of life's ups and downs
But fate's been kind, the downs have been few
I guess you could say that I've been lucky
Well, I guess you could say that it's all because of you

If anyone should ever write my life story
For whatever reason there might be
Ooo, you'll be there between each line of pain and glory
'Cause you're the best thing that ever happened to me
Ah, you're the best thing that ever happened to me

Oh, there have been times when times were hard
But always somehow I made it, I made it through
'Cause for every moment that I've spent hurting
There was a moment that I spent, ah, just loving you

If anyone should ever write my life story
For whatever reason there might be

Oh, you'll be there between each line of pain and glory
'Cause you're the best thing that ever happened to me
Oh, you're the best thing that ever happened to me
I know, you're the best thing, oh, that ever happened to me

Ladies, you may feel this way about your man but does he feel it coming from you? Your man wants to feel this flowing out of your heart, not straining through your teeth! Now, you may feel this way and share it with your man when all the bills are paid on time or you may have become so accustom to it, that you've become callus and cold. You may feel this way when he goes out of his way to do something special for you, but maybe you have started to take his kindness for granted and you don't make sure to show it any more. You may feel it during anniversaries, Valentine's Day or another special celebration, but what about on take-out the trash day or grocery shopping day? The question for you is, do you make him feel that he is the best thing that ever happened to you when you are angry at him, hurt or disappointed?

There is one more song I like to share with you. I don't think the song sold as many copies as these songs Gladys Knight sang. This is the song my then girlfriend and now my beloved wife slipped into my CD player one evening as we were driving down the freeway. We had only been dating a few days and she said to me, "Baby, this song says what my heart feels about you." The song was sung by a talented singing sensation, Shirley Murdock. It is a love song written for Christians called,

"You Are My Ministry"

[Chorus:]
You are my ministry, You are my "help mate to"
When I think about loving myself, I think about loving You
You are my "do me right", my spiritual song in the night
A special part of me, my ministry

[Verse 1:]
Longing to lay my hands on you
Lift you up high when you're feeling blue
Anointed to speak the word over you
When you don't know just what to do
I will be there when things grow cold
My kind of love will heed your soul
I'm at the end of a long hard day,
Waiting to stroke your stress away

[Verse 2:]
Baby come in and shut the door
Drop all your stuff in the middle of the floor
I'm just staring at the clock all day,
Waiting to soothe all your pain away
I am your wife, the woman He sent
Whatever it takes, I'm your instrument
Give everything that you feel inside,
Let it all out, There's no need to hide

[Chorus:]
You are my ministry, You are my "help mate to"
When I think about loving myself, I think about loving You
You are my "do me right", my spiritual song in the night. A special part of
me, my ministry.

No one had ever sung or said words like this to me! I was so used to being the romantic that I didn't realize how bad I, as a man, needed to be romanced by my woman. After experiencing my own failed relationships I could see that this one would be very different. Six weeks after our first date we were married in my living room. She had them play the song in our church wedding later. Now we have been together through ups and downs. The years have taken away some of our youthful looks and we may walk a little slower but we are two of the most passionate lovers you will ever meet.

We still walk into the grocery store holding hands. I open the car door and help her out of the car. I wrap my body around her every night to hold her close an ask God's blessing on her as we drift off to sleep together. She buys me small gifts and surprises me with so many unexpected treats. She told me the other day in her sweet voice, "Baby, you're my best friend...really!" We get up sometimes in the middle of the night and throw on our clothes and take little drives just to be alone and away from the hustle and bustle of life. We love worshipping God together. She calls me several times during the day. I write poems and I email them to her while she's at work. I actually wrote my own song and recorded it just for her and her smile as she listens makes me feel like I am the best singer there ever was; living or dead! Yes, we may be senior citizens in chronological years but our hearts flutter with teenage like puppy love nearly every day! I believe it is because my wife makes me feel that no one in the world is more important to her than me. My wife has lived the lyrics that Gladys Knight sang,

"If I were your woman, You're sweet lovin' woman, If I were your woman...you'd need no other woman."

So don't hold anything back from making your man feel important. Making him feel important makes you important to him. Put down the cell phone. Sometimes turn off the television. Don't answer the door. Carve out some time for your husband and let him know over and over again, that he is the best thing that ever happened to you!

EIGHT

Stop Trying To Change Him

Shelly was 15 years old when Gregory arrived at her school. He was a nice looking young man who was very athletic and had a charming personality. On a few occasions Gregory would get into a couple of fights at school. Then people could see that he could not be bullied around by the tougher kids. Shelly saw him as strong but not aggressive. After the summer break and the kids came back to school Gregory had changed a little. He was hanging out with the tougher boys. He got into a few more fights and even got expelled from school. Gregory asked Shelly to go out once that year and she saw him outside of being a student. She didn't know that Gregory smoked cigarettes and drank. It was no big deal at the time and Shelly had a good time. During that summer they saw each other at the park and a few more places and they were always nice to each other. When their senior year came around Gregory asked Shelly to go out with him. The closer they got to each other Shelly saw that Gregory had a pretty impulsive temper that could flare up without much warning. It was during this time that Shelly began to see why Gregory got into fights. Shelly's friends told her that Gregory was not a good match for her but Shelly pretty much ignored it because she felt that Gregory was fun and exciting when he wasn't angry about something. At 19 years old Gregory got a job and an apartment and asked Shelly to move in with him. Shelly's mom and dad advised her not to do it. Her friends thought it was a bad idea. Shelly also had her doubts because of Gregory's anger issues. She finally decided to move in. Things went well for the first months but soon Gregory seemed to get mad at the least little thing. One day He was fussing at the neighbor because he had blocked Gregory's parking space by parking crooked. Shelly tried to calm Gregory down before things got out of control but before he realized it he snapped and slapped Shelly. Shelly went back into the apartment while Gregory continued to fuss at the neighbor without missing a beat. She told Gregory that she was leaving and moving back to her mom's place but Gregory talked her out of it and said he would change. Shelly stayed there for six more months. During those six months Gregory went to jail twice for assault. He became more and more violent and was finally evicted from his apartment because of the screaming and yelling at neighbors and even Shelly so much. It took Shelly getting slapped again before she finally left him. When Shelly's mom had her home and safe, she asked Shelly why did she stay so long? Shelly said, "I loved him and I thought I could change him."

This story is so typical and it shows how unrealistic many women can be or how off their hopes are as they look at their man. Many women in bad relationships are focused on the problems or the unhappiness and all they try to do is get it fixed so they can feel better. This takes a lot of time, effort and work. In most cases it's impossible without some professional help. When you enter into a relationship you must evaluate your man's imperfections and take an objective assessment of what you and others see in him. Don't rely solely on your feelings because feelings can change and are often misleading. If you are single women desperate to have love and companionship in your life you may be blind to the real truth that could be obvious to everyone else.

If you're already married, then the evaluation period is over. You have to appreciate the gifts and attributes of your man and take responsibility for your own growth. He is who he is.

There may be nothing you can do that is going to change him. In addition to that you must also accept that criticizing him just makes things worse. You may be just letting off some steam but that steam is hot and somebody could be burned badly by it.

The frustration you are dealing with or might face soon in your relationship may not be all about his faults that need to be changed. You may have some growing, maturing and changing to do as well. I know a couple who are constantly in a cycle of frustration because they want each other to change while they continue doing the same things to each other that hinder their growth. In other words they want change but they themselves won't change.

The only time a woman really succeeds in changing a man is when he is a bab y.

~Natalie Wood

You may ask the question, "What if my man really does need to change?" That is a legitimate question and all of us may need to change in some area of our lives. There may be some behaviors that are none productive or even counterproductive. Firstly you must realize that you can't change anyone but yourself. Put it out of your head completely that you can change your man. Secondly, he must want to change. You can make suggestions and you could point out some issues but none of that will cause him to change unless he really wants to. If you really want to help your man make some changes there are a couple of things you must avoid:

1. Avoid Nagging HIM! Let me take the time to share with y ou the small but significant difference between *constructive criticism, destructive criticism* and *productive criticism.*

Constructive Criticism is given for the benefit of the recipient. This means there must be consideration as to how the other person will receive what you say before you say it. You must consider your tone of voice, the timing and even the environment. It is nearly impossible to give constructive criticism when you are angry so you really shouldn't try. Instead wait until you are calm and able to share without clouding the issue with your emotions.

Destructive Criticism is given for the benefit of the speaker. Whether you are able to admit it or not this criticism is all about you. The purpose of the criticism may be legitimate and warranted but the delivery is what is flawed. When the message is about your feelings, your wants or your expectations it is no longer constructive.

Productive Criticism is for the benefit of both the recipient and the speaker. This is more of a positive exchange or dialogue about the hindrances of productivity. It is more like an open analysis or a positive debate. The information is criticized, not the person. The personalities are minimized and the current issues are maximized.

2. Avoid Comparing Him to OTHERS! This is a big mistak
    e of both males and females.

When you compare your man to another man (or woman) you m
ake him feel inferior and inadequate. Men come into relationships and they may have to compete with a woman's father figure whic
h may be a good or bad image. A dear friend of mine was married to a woman who had an abusive father. Everything he did for her had to be filtered through her past experiences with her father. N
eedless to say the marriage didn't last long. People are who they a
re because of a number of factors. Your man may not have the c
ombination of factors that make the person you are comparing hi
m to so you should expect to be nothing more than who he is. As time passes and people go through different processes the experie

nce may bring about adjustments and refinements. To compare y our man to someone else and then expect him to become like tha t person is unfair, unrealistic and will eventually be a great disapp ointment to you both.

3. Avoid Transference. Transference is defined as the uncon scious tendency to assign to others in one's present enviro nment feelings and attitudes associated with significance i n one's early life.

This is a little different than just comparing, but this is when a per son has feelings about a person from their past and they pass the m on to a person they are presently dealing with. For example, a woman was mistreated and fired by a male supervisor on her last job. When she found a new job she had trouble working under th e authority of her new supervisor who was also a male. She did n ot trust him although he had done nothing to warrant the mistrus t. She was distant from him and did no more than her job require d. Later she admitted that her past experience made her hesitant a s to how much she should sacrifice for her new boss. She made h im pay for the way she was treated on her last job. Many people d o the same thing in new relationships. You may be trying to prote ct yourself, but unfortunately it can put a strain on what could be a potentially great relationship. Treat others the way you would li ke to be treated on the merits of your current relationship with th em. Leave the past behind you and allow the good in your situati on to be your strength.

Change is Possible

If you want change, focus on changing you. What can you do better? How can you be better? What can you change in your own mindset that can help the way you process your own situation or your man? Could you be blaming your man for your lack or inadequacies? It is much easier to shift the responsibility on to others than it is to build yourself up in areas where you have a deficit. Changing yourself takes lots of work, consistency and confronting yourself. You have to be open to uncomfortable criticism. It may feel unfair especially if you have areas of insecurity but you must face your faults in order to overcome them.

Let me close this chapter by saying you must be real about where you are in your relationship and the man you are with. When people start having trouble in their relationships they tend to spend more time wishing they had someone else or fantasying about what they wish their man would do or be rather than making the best of where they are. Dreaming about being with someone else or an imaginary person who doesn't exist is very unhealthy for you and your current partner. A healthy relationship is one where both people can be honest and accepting of each other.

Here is a nice quote I read on the internet that sums up this chapter well: *"Love isn't about finding the perfect person but it's about seeing an imperfect person perfectly!"*

NINE

All Men Are Not Created Equal

In our previous chapter we mentioned the danger of comparing and transference. There is another similar danger that needs special attention and that is the danger of generalizing men. This chapter may be more for a single woman who thinks that all men are alike but the information is good for all women.

Generalizing people can be dangerous and cause a person to prejudge. First of all, stop thinking and telling other women that all men are the same; especially if you've had a pattern of bad relationships. Yes, there are many things that are typical or even gender specific, but that is why you hear me say things like "Most men" or Many men" because there will always be exceptions. So I have mentioned expectations and traits that are typical but in this chapter I am speaking more about the fact that every man is an individual with his own unique and specific characteristics, flaws and attributes.

I remember reading something that went like this:

There are different types of men:

1. The ones who are gorgeous, hot and unfortunately they know it just well enough to treat you bad.

2. The ugly ones who treat you like a princess and they are the sweetest a man can be.

3. The hot, sexy, good looking, nice, sweet guys who of course, are gay.

4. The gorgeous, successful, sexy, straight guys who are married and occupied.
SO…WHICH ONE DO YOU CHOOSE

Men are as varied and unique as you women are and putting them all in the same category can do you more harm than good sometimes. Okay, I will admit that there are just some things you are going to see in or get out of most men most of the time. For example:

- We tend to like healthy competition.
- We have a tendency to try to fix broken things.
- Most times we can be pretty logical.
- We can be pretty impatient.
- We don't like to admit when we are lost.

I just want you to know that the levels and slightest variations of these things can make a vast difference in how a man may act or react in certain situations. Read these quotes about men.

Men are like a fine wine. They start out like grapes, and it's our job to stomp on them and keep them in the dark until they mature into something you'd like to have dinner with.

~Author Unknown

There are much easier things in life than finding a good man. Nailing Jell-O to a tree, for instance.

~Author Unknown

What is the difference between men and women? A woman wants one man to satisfy her every need, and a man wants every woman to satisfy his one need.

~Author Unknown

Quotes like these make all men look selfish, inadequate and that it is almost impossible to find a good one. There are some very good men out there. They don't all cheat on their wives and there are actually a few who are sensitive and caring. There are some men who do cry at movies and will open the door for his woman without being asked to do so. You may also run across a man or two who can cook clean and even wash his own clothes. The popular message that many women swear by is that stereotypical men don't do these things but women let me tell you, there are men who do and more.

Many women already have in their minds what they expect in a man. Maybe you were hurt by the last five guys you were involved with. Does it mean number six is also going to hurt you? If you answered "Yes" you could be right and you could be wrong. Just think of how terrible it would be to miss out on a potentially great relationship that you never really gave a chance because you prejudged the man based on someone else's actions. My wife and I met after she had been through three marriages and countless relationships. She was 49 years old when we met. I was the prize that she had been waiting for all of her life and today she says that it was well worth the wait.

The point that I'm trying to make is that men come in many shapes, sizes and designs. There are good men and bad men and some who are somewhere in the middle. Some guys are clean cut fancy dressers and others are happy hobos. Some have looks that only a mother could love while others have inner qualities that far outweigh their appearance. You might get a momma's boy or a momma's nightmare.

Don't assume the worst about a man or the best. People are who they are based on their past experiences, the influences in their life, the way they were raised and the decisions that they make. Consider that it's not that all men are alike, but it could be that you are attracting all of the same kind of men! Manipulative men can spot easy targets and those who are desperate for a relationship might as well write it on their foreheads because they usually tell it in the way the talk, walk and respond.

Maybe you're using the wrong filter to separate the good from the bad or, even worse, you might not be using a filter at all! Filters don't have to be as obvious as paper applications, but a woman should be at least on alert until they know the man relatively well. Here are some signs of a woman with little to no filters:

- Jumping in the bed the on first date.

Although recreational sex is a popular past time these day s for many men and women, it is a most unhealthy thing for a wo man to do as she enters into a new relationship. Show the man th at you are selective and you do have respect for yourself! The bes t plan is to wait until marriage to prove to your man that you con sider your body to be a gift to the man who will be your life partn er rather than it being a life size thank you card for dinner and a movie.

- Taking him to meet family or your kids too soon.

Keep your new relationships private until you are sure yo u can trust him as a part of your life. This is your time to test the waters (filtering). You want to keep the possibilities of collateral d amage down to a minimum just in case things don't go right. Wh en you do decide to bring him around the family, let them be a pa rt of the filtering process. In other words be prepared to listen to their opinions about what they see in him. Sometimes you may be too close to be objective and you need a nonbiased opinion to hel p you see what you can't see or refuse to look at.

- Too trusting, too fast!

You don't put yourself in situations that could be dangero us with a man until you know his heart and his history. It may tak e months before you know him that well. Out of town overnight trips, loaning money or your car, taking on his responsibilities, bu ying large ticket items or expensive things and etc., should only h appen after trust has been earned. Don't let your generosity lead y ou into foolish and unwise choices. Even if you have the money t o spare, it sends the wrong message. Proving his trust and worthi ness is also a good way to scare away most manipulators who thri ve off of the giving heart of a trusting and naive woman.

Filtering may feel at times that you are cutting yourself short as the pickings get less and less. Believe me there are so many women who wish they had taken the time to filter the man who they thought they would be happy with for the rest of their lives only to be left at the alter or in bankruptcy court all alone.

Get to know that man and you will see what he is all about over time. Ask questions about his opinions, his background and the things that he likes to do. Pay attention to his interest, what sport teams does he like and what are his favorite foods. These questions should just start the process of filtering. You may need to go on after this level of filtering and ask his close relatives some questions. Not to dig or probe, but just getting an idea of what they think of him and listen for what is being said as well as what is not being said. I was once in a relationship with a woman. I met her sister who told me about my then girlfriend, "She's just like her father." Well, I should have listened instead of laughing it off. Most of the kids in the family despised the father. He was arrogant and very selfish. He was very difficult to live with and extremely paranoid. The sister who tried to warn me was right and my relationship with my girlfriend was a disaster!

I dated new people after that relationship but now I paid much more attention to what I heard their close friends and relatives say, even if they were joking. Again, it wasn't that I believed every word, but I didn't discount it as being automatically false, especially from an ex-spouse. Now I know that the ex-spouse is off limits for many people but I actually took my current wife to meet my mother and then I took her to meet my ex-wife. I talked to her friends and meant her ex-husband before we got married. Risky? Yes! It worked out well for us.

So the key to treating your man as an individual is all about knowing him very well or at least as well as possible. Then you don't have to assume anything about him. Get an objective opinion if possible. Don't ignore the things you do see and whatever you do, always remember the old saying, "action speaks louder than words!"

TEN

Be His Buddy

This chapter will be nice and short but it is very meaningful. Every woman needs to be her man's best buddy. A man will have a wife at home who is stable and beautiful but have an affair with a woman who is not as attractive as his wife just because she can be his buddy.

A man's buddy is someone who he can tell anything to, can go anywhere with, can spend time with and not be judged, the expectations are minimum, he can be himself and he enjoys spending time with them. Yes, you can see why a man needs a buddy. Girls may need her buddies too but a guy's buddy is his relief from the real world. I can truly say that my wife is my best buddy. I'd rather be with her than anybody else. She loves to talk when I need to talk and she has learned how to be with me even if she doesn't like where I want to go. She will attend an NBA game with me and cheer for my team although she doesn't know the name of a single player. She went to a Major League baseball game with me and when I was done she got up and left with me without a single compliant. She'll watch whatever movie with me that I want to see even if she has no interest in it at all. If I'm in the car on a long drive she is content to listen to whatever music I want to listen to and have whatever discussion with me that I want to have.

Now it may sound like my wife has no interest of her own but she does. She loves talking about spiritual principles and also loves to read when we're traveling. She likes going to second hands stores and yard sales on Saturdays (and makes the occasional stop after work during the week) but she wants to go alone. She also likes going to outlet stores and closeouts by herself. She says she likes to take her time and shop without feeling rushed. That works just fine for me. We both like old school soul and gospel music. She likes the romantic love ballads and I love funky R and B music. What I'm saying is our times together are not a burden for either one of us…that is the best buddy you can have!

The point is that sometimes your man needs to escape from the reality he lives in daily and doesn't want to talk about the kids or the broken garage door that he was supposed to fix last month. When those times happen, you want to be the one he grabs up and says, "Let's get out of here!" because you're his best friend and not be the one he needs a break from. It is true that you do have to discuss that garage door, but if every time you're alone together you pull out a list of things that need to be done and a second list of things that haven't been finished, you are disqualified from being a buddy…you are just a plain old everyday wife.

Your man needs to have fun with you laughing and talking about old times or dreaming about the future. He wants to tell you about the girl who tried to lure him into an inappropriate compromise and how he got out, without you getting angry because it happened in the first place! He wants to talk about the dream for an incredible business or some exciting project without you telling him that he can't afford it, it is impossible or a waste of time. He needs somebody he can be a boy again with and not feel embarrassed or out of line.

An article on the internet written by freelance writer and editor Tielle Webb, where she writes five ways to become your husband's best friend:

- 1. Make time for togetherness. With jobs, housework, kid s and hectic schedules, fun couple time can become a low priority. Move it up the list several notches. Aim to do so mething fun together once a week--once a month at the v ery least. Play a game, eat breakfast at a diner, or start a w ater fight while doing the dishes. Friends have fun togethe r.

- 2. Be patient with your husband. Sometimes he might thr ow his socks on the floor, or drive too fast, or do a gazilli on other things that makes you crazy, angry or frustrated. However, the next time you find nagging words about to exit your mouth, stop and look in the mirror. There is a g ood chance you have flaws, too, and he is probably good at turning a blind eye toward them. Return the favor.

- 3. Listen to him. When both or either one of you comes i n the door at the end of the day, you likely have venting a nd told what you want to do. That is perfectly valid, and v ent you should. Sometimes, though, let him go first. Sit d own next to him and genuinely ask about his day. If he sa ys it was fine, dig a little deeper. Ask him specifics, such a s how a meeting went or what his crazy coworker talked a bout at lunch. Soon he'll be spilling to you and you'll both be feeling closer than ever.

- 4. Show an interest in what he loves. You don't have to at tend every game--although, if that sounds like fun, go for it. Simply pay attention and ask questions about his hobby or passion. Learn some of the lingo, catch team stats on line, or hang out with him once in a while in the garage. You might be happily surprised when he offers to take you to the new antique shop that opened, or inquires about the book your club is reading.

- 5. Be kind to your husband. Make yourself aware of the way you treat him in general. Ask yourself if that is how you would treat your best friend. If so, great. If not, think about changes you can make and look forward to a healthier, happier marriage.

Being you man's best buddy can be a place of honor in his life. It means that he trusts you. It means that he enjoys being with you. It means that somehow you were able to tear down the walls that many men have erected for their own protection and or peace of mind. You may need this more than he does and it will create for you a relationship that many couples long for but just don't know how to make it happen. There is nothing like having a friendship with your man. Like men say that this doesn't happen too often but it should something you strive for and work on. If you're a single woman you should seek friendship before romance. If you're dating a guy you can't have fun with and talk to …he is not the one you want to be your husband because it will come back to haunt you later.

ELEVEN

Fight Like A Man

Honest disagreement is often a good sign of progress.

- Mohandas K. Gandhi

If you want your relationship with your man to last, you must know how to deal with the conflict! I include this chapter on conflict in all of my relationship books and I tailor the content to fit whomever I'm writing the book for at the time. Men do not resolve or fight through a conflict like women do. The "cat fight" full of emotion and wild swinging is a joke to a man. When a man fights he aims and punches both physically and verbally. Domestic conflicts are handled in much of the same way. There is little to no screaming and crying and men never pull off the clothes of his opponent. So ladies, if you want to survive the conflict, you must learn how to "fight like a man."

Too many men and women who say they love each other spend too much time in battle. You cannot start to deal with the other issues, unless we stop here now and discuss the thing we least like to deal with. If you don't learn how to handle the conflicts that you and your man might have, your relationship is doomed from the beginning.

Here's a scenario. You have been preparing all week for a special meal at home for the two of you. There are no children present. The lights are dim and the music is soft and romantic. You went out of your way to make the evening a time to remember. You are having a wonderful dinner together with good conversation and suddenly, the phone rings. You ask your man to let the answering service get it and return the call later. He says, "It may be important." You say, "But our time now is important." He gets up from the table and answers the phone. It's a co-worker and she is trying to hook up her new computer; she calls your man for advice. The call lasts for 20 minutes; to you, it feels like 20 hours. He is eating the food you spent all day preparing and talking to this other woman on the phone. Now you are so angry for the rest of the night. Forget about the nice dinner. You put away the sexy sheer teddy nightgown you had set out for a romantic romp between the sheets with him and pull out the neck-high, ankle-length, floral print flannel gown (not sexy). You're so angry that you go to sleep in front of the TV in the family room with the dog. Your enchanting evening turns into a complete flop. Does this sound familiar?

Conflicts like this occur in the lives of many people. Your loving relationship can abruptly come to an end when conflict arises. This is why the ability to resolve conflict in a relationship is the most important lesson you can learn. Many relationships that become war zones are simply the result of someone never learning how or choosing not to handle conflicts very well. The man in our scenario above made a bad choice, but what was worse, he didn't know how, or chose not to fix it.

The number one reason for relationship break-ups is not money, not communication and not children or in-laws. It is the inability to resolve or manage conflict. Conflict will occur in any relationship no matter how healthy. With the high percentage of dysfunctional families that most of us were raised in, it is almost impossible to believe we can have functional relationships without some help and guidance. Most people simply try to avoid conflict. Some of the reasons are based on fear such as:

1. Fear of the loss of control
2. Fear of intense expression of emotions
3. Fear of exposing true and often hidden feelings
4. Fear of an unexpected outcome
5. Fear of an expected outcome

Let me say, that conflict is an important part of a relationship, and should not be avoided, but *managed* instead. People can learn a lot about each other from conflict. Many lifetime friendships have developed as a direct result of conflict. The conflict removes the mask, which then allows the people involved to see that they have more in common than they may have thought.

True friends become masters of resolving conflicts that come up between them. They learn to accept their friends as they are, rather than always trying to change them. They have come to appreciate what they have, rather than wasting time regretting what they wish they had. This is why it is so important to learn how to appreciate your man.

The greatest cause of conflict in a relationship is when one tries to make the other conform to their standards. Standards could be beliefs, values, methods, opinions or other things. You must learn to let your man have his own opinions, ideas, methods and standards without being challenged by you just because they differ from your own. There may be times when it's best to keep your thoughts to yourself, especially if they are critical of your mate or non-productive. Wisdom knows when those times come. Your mate doesn't have to know every time you have a difference of opinion or you don't like something he or she did. Try to first gauge if it's important enough to bring up.

I once heard a beautiful story from an old preacher I want to share with you. He came home one day from a grueling day at the church where he worked full time. When he walked in the door, his wife gave him a big kiss and welcomed him home. He noticed the house was filled with the fragrance of scented candles that were lit all over the house. His wife told him that this was going to be a special night with no TV or phone calls. She escorted him straight to the dinner table where she had a nice big salad, potatoes, and a perfectly cooked steak waiting for him for dinner. The table was set with a gorgeous candle-lit setting and a bowl of hot lemon scented water where she washed his hands for him. He was amazed at the special attention he was getting. After dinner she insisted that they talk about each other rather than any problems or negative issues. For two hours they talked about how far they had come in life, their plans for the future and their love for each other. When they finished talking they gave each other full body massages, made passionate love and went to sleep in each other's arms. It was a fabulous night!

The next day the preacher got up and went through his usual routine preparing for the day, but when he went to turn on his shaver there was no electricity. He started flipping switches only to realize there was no power in the house at all. He went to the kitchen and said to his wife that the power was off in the house. His wife said, "Yes, it was turned off yesterday while you were at work." He asked, "Why didn't you tell me last night?" She smiled and said, "There was nothing either one of us could do about it then. I decided to make it a special night rather than a stressful night and worry about the power later. I saw that you didn't pay the bill last month. I'll go pay the bill this morning and service will be restored this afternoon." Well, he was late for work that morning as he spent most of the morning showing her physically and sexually how much he appreciated her.

That woman's choice to take a bad situation and make it into something special is one reason why their marriage lasted over 55 years until she died. She could have spent that now memorable evening complaining and expressing her disappointment, but what good would it have done compared to the joy and love they experienced? This is the wisdom we can exhibit during and even before a conflict.

Disrespect is also a major cause of conflicts. Although I will deal with this more in-depth later, I will touch on it briefly here. We should always respect our mates. We may not always understand them or agree with them, but it should never cause us to disrespect them. Disrespect can be expressed in many different ways such as:

1. Sarcasm
2. Insulting remarks
3. Embarrassing comments in public
4. Open rebellion
5. Tone of voice

Another thing that can cause conflict is unclear, or unmet, expectations. Your man may have in his mind what he expects from you. When you do not meet that expectation, the disappointment can result in a major conflict. Having expectations is normal. Not being able to always meet the expectations of your man is also normal. Learning to express disappointment without the need for vindication is the key. Too many individuals use revenge as a way to punish their mate for their disappointment with them. Here's an example:

Wife: Honey, could you go to the store for me?
Husband: Not now. I'm watching the game.
Wife: I can't cook the chicken without oil.
Husband: Why did you wait until the game came on to ask me to go get oil?
Wife: I didn't know we were out until now.
Husband: I guess no one eats chicken tonight. I'm not going to the store until I'm ready!

This is a very selfish response and a childish game that should be avoided no matter how great the temptation. Rather than resolving the conflict, it usually results in more conflict. Understanding, mercy, and compassion should replace revenge.

Always remember, if you are really trying to show your man how much you love him, you would never want to purposely hurt him or see him hurting. For that reason, try to do everything you can to resolve the conflicts you have with your man as quickly as possible. Not because you may be wrong and he may be right, but because you don't want your man hurting over a conflict any longer than he has to.

Flexibility: A Key to Managing Conflicts

The lack of flexibility is what most conflict is all about. Flexibility is necessary in any healthy relationship. People who plan on spending the rest of their lives together should practice it regularly. Most people are flexible within their own comfort zones, but sometimes more flexibility may be required than what you are comfortable with. This is where love, patience, and understanding come into the relationship. The interplay of these will affect the level of flexibility in a relationship. Some women expect flexibility when they need it, but aren't very flexible when someone needs it from them. Flexibility needs to flow both ways in a relationship.

Many people don't really know what flexibility is or understand it. Flexibility means being able to bend or sacrifice for the sake of another. It may mean extending underserved mercy or grace. Flexibility allows room for mistakes and inconsistencies. It doesn't mean that there are no standards or expectations. It simply means there is tolerance when standards or expectations are not met.

People are not perfect and nothing is absolute. No matter how well we put together a plan, there is always the possibility of it going wrong. People who tend to be inflexible are usually perfectionists or just stubborn. The problem with being a perfectionist is that you are never satisfied, because someone always is making a mistake – even yourself. Few people are ever able to reach the unrealistic standards of a perfectionist. When people are flexible, they tend to have more realistic expectations of other people.

Flexibility cuts down on arguments with the end result being a much more harmonious relationship. Conflicts may be unavoidable. If you really want to see them minimized and managed, learn the precious art of flexibility and use it wisely. I'm sure you've heard it said, *"It's not always what you say, but often how you say it."* It's true!

Learn how to vent without purposely hurting your man. Sharing your feelings doesn't mean you shouldn't be concerned about the words you use. Most conflicts begin when one person vents his disappointments to another and in the process they insult and/or disrespect the other person. It is during the venting that people are often belittled and insulted and feel that they must defend themselves or at least stop the verbal onslaught. Be careful how you vent. Also, it would help the person receiving, to try and understand that venting is mostly about emotions.

Sometimes during the venting phase, people say things that they really don't mean to say. Their feelings may be mixed up and their logic may be off. Don't try to hold people captive or judge them based on things said when they were venting. They were most likely intoxicated with their own anger.

- Avoid the following statements at all cost when trying to resolve conflict: *You always...! You never...! Every time...!*

These are generalizations; they might not be true and in most cases they aren't. "Always," "never" and "every time" would mean that there have never been any exceptions.

- Be careful with how you express your concerns to each other: *I wish...! Can't you...! Will you ever...!*

These opening statements usually leave too much room for debate and interpretation and can be a borderline insult. If you have a request, make it clear. Rather than "I wish," ask "Would you please?" Instead of "Can't you try to...?" "Will you please?" Mostly, always be mindful of your tone of voice. Don't ruin a perfectly good apology or explanation with a sarcastic attitude or an insincere tone. You don't want to be misunderstood.

- You cannot read a person's mind: *The reason you did that is...! That's why you...! You think...!*

You may think you know why your man did what he did, but it's only an assumption. Allow your man to tell you what he is thinking, himself. Let him tell you why he did what he did...avoid telling him what you think he is thinking. This in itself is belittling and insulting to most people male or female.

- Don't cloud the main issue with other issues.

That is, of course, when a person uses some other issue as a distraction from the real issue when there is a conflict. People do this to deflect the attention from them. This also causes confusion. Stick to the issue at hand when you're trying to resolve conflict. Save the other issues for another time.

- Don't try to force your mate to discuss it now.

Some people need time to calm down or gather their thoughts about an issue. As long as your mate agrees to another time that works for the two of you, it's okay to postpone the discussion. Indefinite postponement should not be used to avoid a conflict. Work it out as soon as you can. Discuss the issue, forgive each other, if need be, then move on.

- Avoid holding grudges.

If you're married, this is your mate for life, not your enemy. You may be hurt and it may last for a while, but holding a grudge too long can really hurt a relationship. Don't be afraid to sincerely apologize or ask for forgiveness if you are wrong. Don't be like those who just shut down if they are wrong or try to change the subject. Let your mate know you love them enough to want to see the issue resolved. It doesn't matter, if you are the cause of it or not.

- Don't ever compare and say, *My ex-husband did it this way …, My old boyfriend would never…*, or *My dad wouldn't…*, whe n you are trying to resolve a conflict. Never say, *If you we re a real man you would…*

Don't use former relationships as a point of reference or to prove your point. The timing could not be worse to bring this up than in the middle of a conflict. Comparing your current mate to a former relationship is always a bad idea especially when emotions are running high. Reserve those comments for a nice drive in the country or over a game of monopoly -- it's much safer.

THE COUPLES CONFLICT QUESTIONNAIRE

See how well you can discuss the following questions with your man without conflict. If at any point anyone feels a conflict arising, you may call for a 20-second time out. Stop the conversation and take a couple of deep breaths. Together, count to 20 slowly and then resume the conversation.

- On a scale of 1-10 how well do you think we handle our confl icts?

- Remembering the last three conflicts we had, did we handle t hem well? If not, what could we have done to handle them b etter?

- Do we feel free to give our honest feelings about anything as long as we are respectful toward one another and the time is r ight?

- Have we ever or do either of us now lose control when a heat ed conflict arises?

- Is it difficult for either of us to forgive when we have hurt the other? If so, what can we do to help the process of forgiving?

- Do you have constant thoughts of the thing you've been hurt with?

THE COUPLES CONFLICT DECREE

This decree is to help you find the words that express to your lover your sincere heart. Please read the following paragraph one at a time and in turn to each other.

Sweetheart, I am willing to accept your differences of opinions, and in return I ask you to please accept mine. I will try to show my love for you through my respect for you and your individuality. I believe my love for you is stronger than any conflict.

My love, I am willing to accept your right to your own view points that may differ from mine. I see you as an adult, fully capable of living your life without me or my input and consider it a privilege to be your mate; a privilege I will try to never abuse. I believe my love for you is stronger than any conflict.

After you share with each other, think of three things that you each love about the other person that you can say to make them very special to you. Here are some examples:

- I love your honesty.
- You are a good mother or father.
- I appreciate the way you care for me.
- You make me feel safe.
- I appreciate you for listening to me.

THE "PLEASE FORGIVE ME" DECREE

This decree is to help you find the words that express to your lover your sincere heart as you apologize. Please read the following paragraph one at a time and in turn to each other. You may find it necessary to come back here and use these same words during another conflict or disagreement.

I love you deeply, and I know that there are times when I do things that upset you. Although it may seem so, it is not my intention to hurt you in any way. Please forgive me for my lack of consideration at times. I will continue to work on doing better at thinking of how or what I do or say will affect you. I know that my love for you is stronger than this conflict.

Listener 1: I accept your apology.

My dearest, I know that there are times when my imperfections impact our relationship in a negative way. I am offering my apology to you as a symbol of my regret. This may not be enough to erase your hurt immediately, but I hope you will find room in your heart to accept it as a start toward healing. I know that my love for you is stronger than this conflict.

Listener 1: I accept your apology.

Now you both deserve a BIG KISS! Just do it!

TWELVE

Know When To Push And When To Pull Back

Balance is important, but nowhere is it more important than in an intimate relationship between a man and a woman. A good woman must be able to give her man the encouragement he needs, but also know when he needs the strength of his woman. She must pay attention to the signals in the air that suggests the proper time and place for everything. She must know when to push and when to pull back.

A song that actor/singer Kenny Rogers did in a movie called "The Gambler" suggest that pushing and pulling is like a game. The lyrics say,

"You got to know when to hold 'em, know when to fold 'em, Know when to walk away, know when to run.
You never count your money when you're sittin' at the table, There'll be time enough for countin' when the dealin's done."

Women, knowing your place in the life of your relationship with your man is as important as breath itself. You may have heard the term "submission," but didn't understand it fully and many younger women have never seen it in action. Submission in the context of marriage comes from a Bible verse that is found in the 5th chapter of the book of Ephesians,

"Wives, submit to your husbands as to the Lord. For the husband is the head of the wife as Christ is the head of the church, his body, of which he is the Savior. Now as the church submits to Christ, so also wives should submit to their husbands in everything."

This verse is used a lot in Christian marriages to help paint a picture of what a good marriage is supposed to look like. When a woman "submits" to her man it means following his lead and serving him out of the love she has for him. Here is another problem word: "serve." Many women today despise the thought of serving their man, because it has such a negative connotation. Serving another person is a wonderful thing when we know how to push and when to pull back.

Think for a moment about your own picture of a servant. Do you see a broken down slave with chains on his feet and a ring in his nose? Do you see a person who must be beat into submission to the point in which they have no will of their own? This is not the picture I want to see. I prefer the picture of the classy "maître d" (short for *maître d'hôtel*, in the original French, literally "master of the hotel"). The maître d' in the grand hotels may be in charge of the "front of the house" operations and is very helpful to guests. They supervise staff and make sure everything is running smoothly. In large eloquent restaurants he or she is often responsible for the overall dining experience including room service and buffet, and customer satisfaction. This is a servant who finds pride and dignity in serving people. When I have seen these servants in action it is almost humbling to watch them smile at some of the most obnoxious customers.

They go beyond the call of the duty to see that a person's needs are met satisfactorily. They work with a sense of self-accomplishment and internal satisfaction for what they do. This is the person you wish you could take home with you! This high paid professional servant is the same servant a mother needs to be with her children and a wife needs to be with her husband. If she feels like a poor slave or forced prisoner, she is doomed.

Being submitted to your man does not mean blind obedience, but a following that comes from a loving and caring relationship of trust, concern and mutual esteem. A good man is a servant as well. He sacrifices his desires for the sake of his family and specifically for his wife by serving her until the time that only death will separate them.

For a good wife, submission means gladly putting your man first. This is how you pull back. You could have it your way, but you put his desires in front of your own willingly. Another way of pulling back is to honor and respect him even when he is wrong. Seeing your man make a mistake does not give you license to tear him down. Pull back and recognize that when he is wrong is the time he needs to know that you love him. That is when he needs to know that his world is not about to end. I have seen far too many cases of women who never have an encouraging word for their man. They demand, criticize, compare and offer plenty of threats, but rarely or never have an honoring or respectful thing to say.

Let's talk a little more about "pushing." In our modern Western culture, bashing and ridiculing men has almost become a normal thing to do. Knowing how to push is very important. Pushing may mean that you find something nice to say to and about your man at least once a day, even if you have a bad disagreement. Pushing may mean that you encourage him to pursue his dreams when he's ready to give up trying. Pushing may mean that you make it your business to make him think that he is the greatest guy in the world, even if the bills can't get paid.

Knowing when to push is just as important as knowing how to push. You don't want to push your man to go after his dreams of a college education when he may need to take any job he can get at that moment and go to college later.

The best part of "pushing and pulling" is knowing that it is all about the timing.

"There is an appointed time for everything. And there is a time for e very event under heaven -
A time to give birth, and a time to die;
A time to plant and a
time to uproot what is planted."
- Ecclesiastes, 3:1-2

Timing is very important. Sometimes the issue of when y ou say it is more important than what you have to say or even ho w you say it.

As I said in an earlier chapter, you don't have to always ex press your opinion every time you have a thought. Think about th e thought you have, the time you want to deliver the thought and the impact it will have on your man if you say it. Is what you feel you have to say really worth it? When you say, "I just want you to know how I feel," do you really think he doesn't really know how you feel when he looks at that expression of total disgust on your face? Based on the outcome, could you have said the same thing at another time? Maybe you could have or should have just pulled back!

The issue of pulling back and pushing can be applied in m any areas of your life. Your relationship with your man should be

at the top of your list of priorities. Learn how to let pulling back a
nd pushing with perfect timing and the right servant's hearts can
bring peace and harmony to your relationship!

THIRTEEN

Show Your Man Appreciation

Everybody wants to feel appreciated no matter what their gender may be. I believe that one of the best ways to keep anything is to show your appreciation for it. Sometime we take for granted the good things that we have. Men who are good providers, fathers, protectors, care givers and even husbands need to be told in more ways than one that they are appreciated. Sometimes we can be so critical of not having things as perfect as we would like them to be and fail to see all the good that surrounds us. Your man may not clean the house like you, he may snore like a pig, he might be unemployed or a workaholic, but he needs to be appreciated for the good things he does.

Let me tell you a story I heard. Laura was a 27 year old woman who had three kids. She was married to Kenny, a 28 year old painter. Kenny was a pretty average guy who did what he was supposed to do with his life. He went to work every day and came home every night to his family. He was taught by his father to take good care of his family, which he did the best he could. He occasionally brought home some treats and took them out to the movies maybe once a month. He loved his wife Laura and treated her well. Laura had a part time job at the cleaners working a couple hours in the evenings and some Saturdays, but stayed at home most of the day to care for the house and kids. Their life seemed to be going okay. One day Laura noticed that Kenny had started coming home later than usual and asked him why. Kenny said that he was stopping by the coffee shop on the way home to get a cup of coffee. At first Laura didn't pay it any attention. She knew Kenny was a faithful Christian man who loved his kids and she hated to think anything else could be wrong, because they had a good relationship.

One day Laura picked up one of Kenny's dirty shirts to take it to the cleaners and a picture fell out of the pocket. Laura was devastated as she looked at the picture and it was a picture of Kenny with a beautiful young woman. Laura was in total shock as her mind started racing and wondering who could this woman be. As Laura looked closer she could see in the background that the picture was taken in a coffee shop. The girl in the picture had on an apron, this lead Laura to believe that she probably worked at the coffee shop. For a moment Laura was comforted, after all Kenny told her he was getting some coffee after work. But then Laura thought, "What if he's getting more than coffee?" Her imagination started running wild and she began to cry. She asked herself, "How could this happen?" She thought they were happy and everything was so good. Then she thought about how routine everything was in their relationship. She thought that maybe this girl was probably more exciting than she was. Laura started comparing herself with the girl and looked in the mirror. Now was disgusted, because she had picked up a few pounds and felt that maybe her weight was the problem.

Laura spent the rest of the day wondering what had she done wrong to push her husband away. What Laura was going through was what many people go through after the burial of a close loved one. They ask themselves the question, "Did I tell them I appreciated them enough?" This is where Laura was and this was a good question for her to ask herself. She knew she was a good wife and they had a great relationship, but she also knew that her one area of weakness was not showing her appreciation.

She thought back to a day when Kenny had to work on a special project on his job that required him to work overtime for a few weeks. He had come home and fell on the couch exhausted from the 12 hour day. Laura had been out with the kids shopping. The kids gave her a rough time that day so she was also exhausted when she came home. When she walked in and saw Kenny asleep on the couch she shouted at him sarcastically and said, "You get to sleep and I get to shop with these crazy acting kids today!" Kenny said in an angry response, "Will it make you feel better if I add shopping to my 12 hour day? Could you show a little appreciation for what I do?" But she dismissed the incident back then thinking it was just a moment of anger that all couples experience from time to time. This memory was now loud and clear in Laura's mind.

There was another issue that Laura didn't talk about too much that was also coming to her mind. Laura felt in her heart that she was a hard worker in her home and that if anyone deserved appreciation, it was her. Kenny was great about bringing his wife flowers and other special gifts to show his appreciation to her, but Laura felt that Kenny really didn't need it or even wanted it for that matter. Now she was questioning her reasoning and regretting the countless missed opportunities to say thanks rather than complaining so much. Laura had to now admit that her feelings were very selfish and if she had a chance to do it over again she would do things different. She decided to go find her husband and beg for another chance.

Laura raced as fast as she could to the coffee shop where Kenny goes after work and saw him sitting alone at a table in the back of the room. It wasn't long before Laura found out that the beautiful young woman in the picture was the daughter of the owners who was leaving for college the day the picture was taken. She considered Kenny to be one of her easiest customers to serve, because he orders the exact same thing every day and asked her mother to take the snap shot. It was a friendly gesture with no ill intent.

Laura's panic attack turned out to be a false alarm, but it made her realize that she was taking her husband's goodness for granted. This can happen to the man and the women, so both need to be aware of this important basic need. Here are a few things to remember:

1. Say "thank you" for even the small things.

2. Don't base your appreciation on your feelings. You m ay be upset about something he did that you don't ap preciate, but don't let that cancel out the good things you do appreciate.

3. Men love gifts as much as you do, but they like functi onal gifts. Flowers don't mean much to most men, bu t here is a short list of gifts you may want to consider for your man:
   - Magazine of his favorite subject
   - Multi use pocket tool
   - Gift card to his favorite store
   - Tickets to a sporting event he likes (good seats should be considered)
   - Something for his car or truck
   - Things to help him organize his things
   - Movie tickets to see a movie he likes
   - Anything you know your man really likes

Showing that you appreciate your man is crucial. As we saw in our story with Kenny and Laura's home, you don't always know if a person feels unappreciated. Some men feel that if they confess that they don't feel appreciated it is a sign of weakness. Let me say this again, men need to feel that they have worth. To say "I don't feel appreciated" is the same as saying "I don't feel important to you." That is a hard thing for many men to admit or even suggest.

Give your man what he needs from you to help him feel that he is needed **by you**. Let me again emphasis the phrase "by you!" He needs to hear it from you. Many men may sound powerful in their place of status and importance outside the home, but your man is who he is when there are no crowds and no staff. This is one of the reasons why so many female secretaries are able to steal the hearts of so many married bosses unintentionally. The secretary knows him behind the scenes and away from his show of power. She hears his complaints and knows all his enemies. Her job may technically be answering the phone, typing and filing, but if she wants to keep that job she must be prepared to lift him up when he's down. She must know what he likes and how he likes it and all of the things that I have written earlier. In most cases the secretary is with her boss for 8 to 10 hours a day and she must be his biggest fan or she'll be fired and replaced. She serves him and cheers for him; she protects him as a screener from the unwanted world. These secretaries have enormous amounts of power solely based on the day to day relationship they have with the boss.

You should not attempt to compete with a secretary or bring yourself to her level; you only need to understand what she understands. She understands that her boss needs her to appreciate him where he is and meet his needs. Any woman who understands that as a fundamental purpose in the marriage will go far. If you want the marriage to last long, do everything reasonable to appreciate the good that you have in your man. Don't focus on his mistakes. Don't complain about what you wish he would do. Remember, you can't change him, but you can create an atmosphere that makes him want to change.

Think about those traits that make him stand out above other men you could have been with that made you want to be with him. Come down off your pedestal and show your man that you realize he could have selected another woman. Humble yourself and let him know that his faithfulness to you is appreciated. His looking out for you is appreciated. His being a good father or provider or protector or whatever he is not taken for granted. This advice is worth millions, but costs as little as saying, "Thank you!" "You didn't have to do that for me!" "I really appreciate the things you do for me!"

Appreciate your man before someone else does and/or does it better than you. He may not have or want a sexual affair with another woman, but he might be so hungry for appreciation that he slides right into her arms without even realizing that you pushed him there. Is he justified for doing it? No, but it happens! Is appreciation a guarantee that it won't happen…no, but it sure cuts down that chances that it will. It doesn't matter how old he is, how he looks, how much money he makes or how good he is or is not at anything every man needs to know that he is appreciated. Your job is to make sure that he gets that from you more than anyone else!

FOURTEEN

Look Good For Your Man

The song says "beauty is only skin deep." The title of this song may be true, but beauty is important to men. Now we mentioned in an earlier chapter that men see more than a pretty face, but what are men attracted to?

Paris Hilton said, *"No matter what a woman looks like, if she's confident, she's sexy."*

To a certain degree Paris is right because for many men confidence is very sexy, but while it may look sexy the next quote must also be considered,

The average woman would rather have beauty than brains, because the average man can see better than he can think.

~Author Unknown

The average woman I know doesn't have a problem keeping up their appearance. The vast majority of women are clean and present themselves in a way that is pretty impressive. But this section is not about the way I see the average woman. By the time I see a woman, most of them have prepared themselves to be in the public. They have everything just right for the public to view their perfectly made up eyes and their carefully cut and styled hair. The clothes they wear are all coordinated and fit them just right, but that is for the public. That is all nice, but it may not be how you dress for your man at home in private.

I'm not saying that a woman needs to be this picture of glamour and beauty when she wakes up or is cleaning her house or just relaxing for that matter. I am saying that your husband would like to see the woman he fell in love with look the way she did when she grabbed his attention and he couldn't keep his eyes off of you, occasionally at home just for him.

It doesn't matter that you may have gained some weight or you have a little sag now. The point is the effort you put into impressing your own husband. When I bring this up to some women the first thing they say is, "He doesn't dress up for me!" Let's be real about this. Most men only "dress up" for special occasions or events like church or the job because they have to. They will go to the store in the same thing they wear around the house. Many women will get "dressed up" to make a 5 minute run to the cleaners! When I tell my wife to come and go to the hardware store with me she says, "Let me go get dressed." I say, "Baby, you look just fine!" She says, "I don't know who I might run into and I don't want anyone to see me in public like this." Okay, I must admit, when she comes out of that room she is looking great, but that was not for me!

I think most men would faint if one day they saw their lady spending an hour or two getting "dressed up" and when he asked, "Where are you going?" His woman said, "Nowhere. I am getting dressed just for you." This is the point of this chapter, to raise your awareness of something that can easily be taken for granted. Your man needs to see you as the beauty you are in your comfortable and "uncooked" (raw) natural self. But there are other times when he wants and needs to see his queen, your highness, in her royal garb just for him.

I like to ask women, "What is your husband's favorite dress or his favorite color on you?" I ask that because a lot of men don't get the opportunity to choose what their woman will wear, because the woman has already decided what she is going to put on. If my wife asked me what she should wear, my answer would probably be, "I don't care." This is because in my opinion she looks good in everything she wears. My point is a possible shift in thinking at times to dress and be beautiful for your husband rather than just for yourself or the public. I have a few pointers that may be a help to you.

1. Your favorite sweats or flannel pajamas maybe warm, but they are not sexy.
2. Even if you can't afford to get your hair done regularly, every day shouldn't be a bad hair day.
3. Most men like the feminine side of you (please try to look like a woman).
4. Don't give up on your looks even if you're dissatisfied with yourself.
5. Women who work hard to keep themselves up usually get the most attention from their man.
6. Men like women in all shapes and sizes. If your man chose you, he probably likes your size even if you don't.
7. A smile is the most beautiful accessory any woman can wear.

Flowers... are a proud assertion that a ray of beauty out values all the utilities of the world.

~Ralph Waldo Emerson, 1844

In researching for this chapter I found a nice article on the internet I thought you would enjoy. There was no author to credit and it doesn't seem to be scientifically exact, but you can be the judge of its worth. The title of the article is:

10 Natural Steps to Being Beautiful on the Inside and the Outside

1. Drink plenty of water. (Apart from hydrating your body it does wonders for your skin!)
2. Make this delicious nourishing facemask with 2 Tbsp milk powder, 1 Tsp Cocoa powder, 1/2 tsp yeast and 1 Tsp yogurt. Mix all of them and apply on your face and wash off after 20 min with lukewarm water followed by cold water to find a completely rejuvenated you!!
3. Catch up on at least 8 hrs of beauty sleep.
4. Every morning cleanse your face by rubbing a cotton ball dipped in milk. Not only will this make your skin soft it will also help in reducing blemishes and improve patchy skin.
5. Once a week pamper your body with this homemade seductive body mask. Blend together 1 teacup of fruit (avocadoes, strawberries, banana, papaya anything that pleases you!) with 1/2-cup milk cream. Add 1-cup sugar and juice of 1 lemon. Massage on your body and let it be for 10 min and shower!! Now enjoy the feel of your fresh honeydew soft body!
6. Add a few drops of glycerin (available at any pharmacy) to your usual hand cream and apply it lavishly on your hands and feet and find your tips and toes glowing the next morning.
7. Exercise regularly. You need not have to necessarily t

ake out time to make it to the gym every other day jus t simply energizing your daily activities can make a wo rld of difference. While in the kitchen, switch on the music and groove with the music while you cook som e tasty healthy salads or dinner.

8. Think positive and act positive. Reach out to others w ith your positiveness and see a world of difference. Y our feelings and emotions are contagious to all those around you so make sure to exhibit the same behavior to others that you expect from them.

9. Smile as much as you can. There is no point brooding over things you have no control on, so better still thin k of alternatives to set them right instead of thinking why they didn't go right for you.

10. Respect others and what they do! It may sound philos ophical, but it is actually the inner you that has a great impediment to make a more beautiful you from outsi de.

So be beautiful inside and you'll really be pleased to see a more be autiful you in the mirror every day! And believe me you really wo uld never have to go about browsing 'blogs' for beauty tips again!

FIFTEEN

Be A Bra For Your Man (lift, support, and separate)

Back in the 60's and the 70's I remember watching a popular TV commercial by a company that made bras. This particular bra was called a "Cross your heart bra." The commercial always advertised that the bra's strongest features were that it "lifts, supports and separates." Being a man or a boy at that time, I had no idea what that meant or why it was needed in a bra, but as a woman you probably understand the importance of these features much better than I do since I've never had a need to wear a bra. I am going to try to explain how I think the features of this bra are exactly what your man needs from you.

Lifting is all about encouraging. When your man is feeling down for any reason, he needs your help. He may not act like he needs anything and probably won't ask for help at all. He may reject your offer to do anything, but one thing he most likely never rejects is your encouragement. When a man is feeling discouraged, it is usually connected to feelings of failure. Most men accept responsibility for themselves and family, if they have one with little difficulty. Accepting responsibility doesn't mean that they do everything right, but they do try. When something goes wrong most people look for someone to blame and many people blame themselves. A good man will take responsibility for the failure (he may not admit it) and you see a guy withdrawn with his head hung down, he doesn't want to talk (unlike the typical woman) and he may go straight to his computer, sports or video games to escape.

Some men are very good at hiding their disappointments while others let the whole world know. Many men internalize their hurt and mask it with laughter or something else. Showing emotion is a sign of weakness for most men and you, as a woman, may think your guy is just fine or that deal that went bad didn't really hurt him too bad. If you know your man well you will be able to tell when he needs to be lifted up. He may get quiet or seem to shut down. That may be because he is thinking about his next move he needs to make or he is replaying in his mind what happened so he won't make the same mistake again. This is not the time to ask your man how does he feel or any other questions for that matter. You may think that he needs a kiss or a hug. It may be okay to do that, but don't expect a response.

As we have said before women and men are quite different and they need different things. What may lift you up when you're down may irritate him. You need to find out what your man needs rather than be insulted, because he didn't respond to your kiss or he's not talking to you. Read this short story about a couple and the night they hit an unexpected bump in the road of their marriage.

One evening Kristie saw her husband John sitting alone by the pool and went out to find out what was wrong. She knew something was wrong, because whenever something is wrong this is what he does. Calmly she asked, "John is everything alright?" At first John didn't move. He just kept staring at the sparkling water in the pool as if Kristie never said a word. Kristie knew her husband and rather than badgering him until he responded, she walked over to the back of the chair he was sitting in and gently began to massage his neck and shoulders. After about five minutes John finally opened his mouth, "Well, I blew my temper at work today and yelled back at the boss in front of everybody. I might get fired. Kristie quietly kept massaging her husband for a moment and then with a loving and confident whisper said, "You've been under a lot of pressure lately. We'll work it out together no matter what they decide. Just relax right now."

What Kristie did was "lift" her husband! She resisted the temptation to ask about all the details. She didn't make a judgment on who was right and who was wrong. She recognized that he didn't need to talk until he was ready. She helped him relieve the stress with a massage, then gave him respect and reassured him that she was going to be there no matter what happened with the job.

Kristie also knew what her husband needed to hear that would lift him up. Remember women your husband may not need to hear what you would need to hear. Many men just don't hear words such as love, cute, adore, sweet, treasure, special and etc., unless it is connected to romance or sex. Words that express emotions can be difficult for some men to say and they rarely have any connection to his heart. However men do respond to words that convey respect, and worth. Tell a man that you admire or that you are impressed with him. Use words that make him feel that he is important to you.

Then there is the issue of *Support*. Support does not mean that you agree with everything your man says or does. It means you stand with him as he does what he does. I love watching those movies where the captain has to make a life or death decision for the right cause. He knows the risks are high and there is a great chance that they might fail, but then he asks the question, "Who's with me?" There is the pause and then you see a few faithful "supporters" step up and volunteer. The supports are not always saying I agree, they are saying I am willing to believe in what you believe in. I am willing to give my life to help you do what you believe you can do (all men love these kind of stories). Even the guy who is absolutely opposed to the strategy will sometimes shake his head and say, "Let's do it." They stand together, because of the cause they all believe in. They go up against incredible odds, because they all support the same cause. Men look at a person who thinks about his self-preservation over the cause as a wimp or weakling. When you can sacrifice yourself for a cause bigger than yourself; a good man considers that honorable.

You're on a journey with your man, but you must let him do the driving. You must resist the temptation to grab the steering wheel or be a back seat driver. You can't gripe and complain the whole trip, but do what you can to make the trip as pleasant as possible.

When you support your man even when you don't see where he is going it shows him that you are worth honoring!

Support him by doing what Kristie did when she said, *"We'll work it out together no matter what they decide."* This translates to rank in a man's mind. A statement like that means that he out ranks his opponent in the eyes of his woman. This is the language (Man Talk) that will connect to your man's heart. Unfortunately, most women don't speak this language. Therefore, they are often left disappointed and frustrated, because they can't get their man to talk to them.

Finally, there is the issue of *Separate*. The definition for separate is *to keep apart or divide, as by an intervening barrier or space: to separate two fields by a fence.*

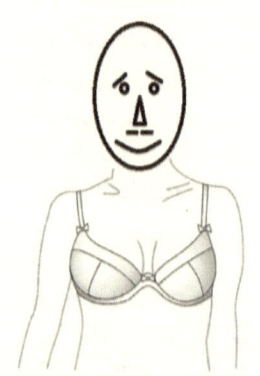

Help your man to feel that when he is with you it is like the old Stevie Wonder song entitled, "You and Me Against the World!" Help him to separate himself from the trials of life and the pressures of people. Help him to feel that his home is a sanctuary where there is peace and safety. Help him to separate from the pull to conform to the expectations of others. It may be at home, but it may also be in the car on a drive, in the park or the beach, in the church or a football game. You don't have to be totally alone to separate. It is all about making your time together as special and inclusive of each other as possible. When my wife and I go to an NBA game together, it is us separating an event for us or in other words…a date. If I really want to watch the game, I watch it on TV!

So my dear lady, being a "bra" for your man is one of the best things you can do for him. I hope that each of you reading this book can grasp the concept that your man needs a woman who can lift him when he's down, support him when he feels weak and alone, and help separate him from the rest of the world if but for a moment of retreat.

One final note: No man wants to be in an intimate relationship with anyone where he feels like he is in competition with. With these three pieces you can bring pleasure into the life of the average man. Lifting, supporting and separating are how a wise and caring woman loves her man.

SIXTEEN

Make The House A Home

Mid pleasures and palaces
though we may roam,
Be it ever so humble,
there's no place like home.

~John Howard Payne

Part of the above quote I have heard for years (there's no place like home), but reading the whole phrase has made me appreciate the little poem even more. I want to take this chapter and really emphasis the need for a woman to make her home as precious of a sanctuary as possible for her man and her family. In most cases you can't do it alone, especially if you and your man are working, but you certainly cannot leave it to chance. You must make it a priority and accept that it will have an influence on your relationship. I know you may feel overwhelmed at times, but this is a necessary component that cannot be taken for granted.

Dr. Rodney Pearson

There is a major difference between a house and a home. A house is a building, but a home is the atmosphere in the house. A home is much more than a house. It is that place where a person lives, spends much of their time, or feels generally comfortable with. Home is the feeling of safety and protection. Home is belonging and family. Home is warmth and security. Someone once said that "Home is where the heart is." Home is not that transient feeling where you know you will be moving on soon. It is not just a place where you just go to poop, eat and sleep.

Making a good home for your man is essential. You and your man may buy the house or lease the apartment but I believe that as a woman, you play a major role in making the house a home. The home should be a reflection of who you are as a family. It should be as comfortable as possible and everyone in the family should guard it like a treasure; starting with you.

Channing Pollock said, *"Home is the most popular, and will be the most enduring of all earthly establishments."*

Some women have difficulty with this, because they may not have been raised in a healthy home environment, so they don't know what a home should look like or feel like.

Joyce Maynard said, *"A good home must be made, not bought."*

So you women must take responsibility for setting a tone of warmth and peace in your home rather than to allow clutter and chaos to take over. Do not think of yourself as a maid or a hired servant, although you may feel like it at times. Think of yourself more as a train engineer of sorts or an airline pilot. You are keeping the vehicle functional, on target and the passengers comfortable.

Diane Mariechild said, *"A woman is the full circle. Within her is the power to create, nurture and transform."*

I love this quote, because it shows the strength that a woman has and what she is able to do with it. A woman is a powerful and influential being and has been given gifts and talents that no man can duplicate.

In an earlier chapter in this book we quoted the following sayings from *Proverbs 21: 9 & 19* *"It is better to dwell in a corner of a housetop, than in a house shared with a contentious woman... It is better to dwell in the wilderness, than with a contentious and angry woman."*

Another quotation from Proverbs 27:15 says *"A continual dropping in a very rainy day and a contentious woman are alike."*

These proverbs should tell us something about the importance a woman plays in either setting up or tearing down the harmony and peace in the home. The aforementioned proverbs use the term *"contentious woman"* and I think we should look deeper into this meaning.

The word contentious means: *to assert a point as part of an argument, inclined or showing an inclination to dispute or disagree, always ready to argue; quarrelsome of or marked by contention provoking or likely to provoke controversy.* Do you think that this kind of personality would make for a comfortable home for any one?

When a home is full of contention, it can be for a few reasons:
1. There could be a power struggle going on. There mus t be give and take which means fair compromise.
2. There could be resentment. This could be, because of blatant or subtle unforgiveness or inconsideration of one or both parties.
3. There could be a conflict in values. What is important

to one is not important to the other.

This list could go on and on. These are issues that should have been worked out before the marriage, but are often over looked for one reason or another.

Since we have used the biblical proverbs to make an earlier point, let me site another biblical writing for you to consider in making your home a comfortable place for both you and your man.

The writing is found in 1 Peter 3. This reference comes from a contemporary easy to read version of the bible called the New American Standard Bible. It reads as follows:

1) In the same way, you wives, be submissive to your own husbands so that e ven if any of them are disobedient to the word, they may be won without a wo rd by the behavior of their wives, 2) as they observe your chaste and respectful behavior. 3) Your adornment must not be merely external—braiding the hai r, and wearing gold jewelry, or putting on dresses; 4) but let it be the hidden p erson of the heart, with the imperishable quality of a gentle and quiet spirit, w hich is precious in the sight of God.

The admonishment from the writer of the scripture suggests that a man's inappropriate behavior can be changed by a woman's gentle and respectful behavior. It also refers to a very important point about appearance saying, *"Your adornment must not be merely external…'*External appearance seems to be the focus of many women even from childhood with the prissy, cute dresses and hours put into styling hair. Little time is put into the development of what the writer calls the *"imperishable quality of a gentle and quiet spirit…"* The word "spirit" here would refer to internal temperament of the woman.

Contentiousness seems to be passed down from generation to generation as girls watch their mother contend with their fathers, other men and even other women. The battle between two women, called a *"cat fight,"* is acceptable entertainment in many settings and cultures and it should not be a surprise that this "internal temperament" in women is found in many homes.

So far we have mostly talked about how you and your attitude can contribute to making your house a beautiful home, but you must also be concerned about the physical part of the home. You don't have to live in a mansion or some country villa to have a comfortable home to live in. Your small apartment, a compact house or mobile home can be as pleasant and wholesome as any other place, if you take the time to make it that way. Be creative, look at magazines like Home and Garden to get decoration ideas and hints. Go to places like do it yourself stores like Lowes and Home Depot to get interior design ideas. A picture hanging here and there or a change in the table cloth or shower curtain can make all of the difference in the world and it doesn't have to cost you a ton of money. You can make your home your home just by using tasteful accents and carefully chosen accessories.

Now let me warn you ahead of time your man may not even notice the small or drastic change you make. He may walk right past the fresh flowers you bring in and he may not say a word about the new linen or matching blankets on the bed, but if it helps him to feel more at ease or more relaxed in his home, that is what you really want and it should be your ultimate goal. Don't ruin your efforts and get angry, because he didn't mention anything about all your hard work to "fix things up." I have seen too many women angry, because their man didn't give them the accolades and praise they felt they should have gotten for doing what they should have wanted to do for themselves anyway. It's your home too! If he doesn't say a single word of appreciation, it's okay. Just give yourself a pat on the back and know that you did what you could do to make your house a better home. Learn and remember this: self-satisfaction is longer lived than a pretentious parade in your honor.

Here are a few more suggestions that may be helpful in setting a peaceful atmosphere in your home for your man:

- Light smooth music in the background.

Sometimes turn the TV off (never do this if you know he wants to watch a game or regular scheduled program without his agreement). Find soothing instrumentals, smooth jazz or whatever your preference may be. It doesn't always have to be romantic or even instrumental. Some people like gospel and there are even recordings of waterfalls, birds and crickets chirping, raindrops, streaming rivers and others.

- A pleasant smell like scented candles and other aromatic aids.

Often after cooking a meal on the stove or microwave the house may smell like fish or bacon. (Some men have no problem with the smell of food, but it may bother you.) The kids may burn popcorn or the smell of bleach or cleaning solution may be dominated. If weather permits open the windows when cooking. Allow fresh air to flow through your house when possible.

- Set appropriate lighting.

Sometimes the lights should be dim and or a bit subtle when trying to set an atmosphere for calmness or tranquility. Fireplaces and candles are great for romance. I found a DVD that actually has several fireplaces that continuously burn and sound like a real fireplace. My wife and I have often cuddled up and fallen asleep with a crackling fireplace burning in the background and no mess to clean up in the morning, thanks to that convenient DVD!

- General cleanliness.

Nobody, man or woman, wants to live in a cluttered and/or dirty environment. Do whatever you can do to help clean and organize your home. Partner with your man and make a plan that works best for the both of you. If you are single, you need to understand that if you keep a dirty house before marriage, you will most likely do the same after marriage, so start cleaning now. Children always make a mess, so you must teach them to clean up behind themselves early.

Dear precious woman, look for ways to be a peacemaker in your home. Create an atmosphere that is clean and wholesome for all who enter. Do this with consistency and sincerity and I believe it will be another thing to please your man and keep him that way!

SEVENTEEN

Kill The Control Freak In You

Many men don't see a woman when they see a strong and/or independent women they automatically see a control freak. A woman who is a control freak is usually just a very insecure woman. In order for that person to feel some level of security, they must know what's going to happen, what they need to make it happen, when it is going to happen, how it is going to happen and who's going to make it happen as often as possible. That person may not admit that they are a control freak, but if they smell, look and act like a control freak…they probably are a control freak!

So let us make it plain, men and women both can be control freaks. The difference is that most women who are control freaks are not really looking for control that comes with power, but they need to feel as secure as possible. This is why women who are control freaks don't really realize it until a man points it out.

Dr. Rodney Pearson

For years many women have been told that they were not as good as men, didn't deserve to be treated as equals, even if they work as hard or even harder than men all the while they were the ones keeping things in order for their men behind the scenes. To make matters worse, some of these same women saw that as soon as they put certain things in the hands of a man it often fell apart.

When you take control (or leadership which equates to worth) away from a man, that man feels disrespected, disempowered and emasculated. This affects his self-esteem and he either becomes weak as a leader or may go in the other direction and become abusive to feel some sense of power. Some even act out and/or find other things to numb the feelings of inadequacy like, over working, physical exertion, drugs or inappropriate sexual relationships. There may be many places a man may feel his place of leadership has been taken, but is devastated when it happens in his own home with his wife. Many women don't know when or how they take control away from a man or take control of a man which are two different things. Let me tell you the story about Andrew and Angie.

Andrew was a young man who thought he found the love of his life in Angie. He was a nice looking, hard worker and could be a very loving man. Angie was a beautiful and sexy woman. She was fun and full of life and laughter. They were both young and were ready to embark on a new life as husband and wife. When they first got together Andrew would attempt to do something and Angie would suggest an alternative way of doing it. Andrew would consider it to be a helpful gesture and really appreciated the help of his new bride. During the preparations for the wedding Andrew noticed that Angie always had to have certain things certain ways. Andrew went along with it feeling that it was her first wedding and she was entitled to have the things that pleased her for that special day. After the wedding Angie had a lot of ideas for the new apartment. Then she wanted a certain car.

When she got pregnant Angie had to have certain foods and the house had to look a certain way. As time went on Andrew noticed that everything was all about Angie. Soon Angie was in charge of the bank account and paid all the bills. She selected the food and dressed the family to her liking. Andrew went along with everything, but after being with Angie for five years he realized he was simply a pay check for Angie. Angie told him everything from what to eat, to when he could have sex with her. When Andrew was promoted on his job, he was assigned a secretary. The secretary was an average looking lady, no comparison to Angie and about 10 years older. When Andrew was at work, he would tell his secretary what to do and was clearly in charge. At home Angie was always in charge and had everything under her control. Angie loved and respected her husband, but she ran him and the home. One day Angie called the office where Andrew worked and found out that Andrew and his secretary both had the day off. It didn't take long before it was revealed that Andrew was having an affair with his secretary.

What eventually surfaced was that Andrew's secretary admired his strength and abilities to manage the company. Andrew felt strong and appreciated how his secretary looked to him for direction and company related directives. She wouldn't do a thing without first going through her boss Andrew while Angie never asked Andrews opinion about anything. When the gossip spread people asked, "How could he mess around with that older woman over his beautiful wife?" The answer was simple. Andrew's secretary made him feel like he was a capable and competent man while he was at work. He wasn't questioned about his decisions. He was admired and trusted. He was looked up to as a leader and everyday his secretary served him eagerly and faithfully. Angie made him feel like a visitor in his own home. She was task oriented and could run all of the operation of the house without his help at all.

Angie didn't realize that she was doing too much and taking away her man's sense of self-worth at home. She thought she was being a good wife…and she was. She just wasn't aware that Andrew needed his ego stroked and lifted from his wife.

Okay, I can admit that most men are egomaniacs, but I believe that is connected to our tendency to lead, protect and provide for our families. There has to be some high level of self-confidence to do that effectively. As we have shared with you earlier there's nothing wrong with boosting your man's ego. It makes him feel good about himself and if a good woman knows how to make him feel good, he would be a fool not to want to keep her around and keep her happy. Don't take him for granted, because if you don't do it, someone else just might beat you to it. It doesn't mean that your man is a weakling waiting to be swept away by anyone who will pay him a little attention.

Most men are actually are attracted to independent women, but they don't want to be controlled by them (at least not outside of the bedroom).

A contributing writer wrote the following in an article about stopping controlling behavior on the EHOW.com website that I thought could be helpful:

1. Ask yourself why you want to stop being controlling. Write down in a journal how being controlling is a pr oblem in your life.
2. Increase your awareness of when you are controlling. Whenever you find yourself acting this way, note it in your journal and write down what the situation was, w hat you were thinking and feeling, what you said or di d that was controlling, and the effect it had on others. Do this for a few weeks.
3. Read over your self-observations, thinking about why you are controlling. What does this behavior do for y

ou?

4. Notice if there are any patterns that can show you wh y you act this way. Are there attitudes, expectations or beliefs you have about how others should be, how life should be, and so forth? Write them down.

5. Decide if you are willing to challenge these underlying attitudes that fuel your need to control.

6. Think of an alternative attitude or perspective you co uld take when you get the impulse to control. (This wi ll often be the opposite of what you came up with in s tep 4.) Examples might be: "I can trust others to do t hings," "There are more ways than my way," "Connec ting with others is more important than controlling ot hers."

7. Think about alternative ways you could act, if you too k on these new perspectives. For example, you might be silent, listen or let others do it their way.

8. Write down these new perspectives and behaviors an d place them where you will see them regularly - for e xample, on your car dashboard, mirror, computer scre en or refrigerator.

9. Try to catch yourself anytime you find yourself being controlling and stop yourself as soon as you can. Rem ind yourself of the alternative attitude and try to practi ce the alternative behavior.

No one wants to feel controlled or suppressed by another person. You want your man to look forward to coming home, not being afraid of not coming home. Believe it or not men can also be abused by women. So sister, learn to relax and if you wonder are you controlling or not, ask your man. If he says "a little" or a definite "yes," don't blow it off or slam your man for being honest. Go back to the beginning of this chapter and read it again carefully. You can be free from the controlling behavior, but it takes work, honesty and willingness to accept correction from the one you're trying to control.

EIGHTEEN

Love Your Man Unconditionally

Unconditional Love

A treasure to be cherished,
A gift from God above;
Is the beauty of a friendship,
Touched by unconditional love.
A love that asks no questions,
Believes in all the best;
Never doubting, ever trusting,
Withstanding any test.
A love that weathers any storm,
And yet that love still stands;
Through the very darkest hour,
It still reaches out a hand.
There in that hand the sweetest gift,
That you can give a friend;
A heart that cares, a love that shares,
That will be there till the end.

A treasure to be cherished,
A gift from God above;
Is what I share with you my friend,
An unconditional love.

I found this cute, yet powerful, poem by Allison Chambers Coxsey and just had to reprint it.

Love is without question one of the deepest and expressive emotions that any person male or female can have. It is more than just a caring feeling of affection that you feel for another person, yet it does include those feelings. Ask a group of people and everyone will have their own definition of what love is. Regardless of what anyone's opinion about love may be, when the subject about intimate love between you and a man and spending your lives together come up, there are only two kinds of love that need to be considered, conditional love or unconditional love.

Unconditional love is the most genuine love there is and it means to love someone regardless of the loved one's qualities, actions or their ability to love you in return. One good example of unconditional love to look at is a mother's love for her newborn baby. The mother is willing to do anything for her helpless infant. She cares for the child for many sleepless hours in their sickness. She gives sacrificially for the well-being and safety of the child, yet the child can do none of this in return for the mother. She doesn't look for monetary compensation of any kind. Most women are very familiar with this kind of love.

Most people don't have a clue about the power of real unconditional love, because there is so much fake love around them every day of their lives. For a while I worked in the movie industry in Hollywood and I never saw so much smiling and hugging by people who hated each other or only wanted to secure a job. The same thing happens in politics and in the marketplace.

The best way to know the difference between what is counterfeit or what is not is by studying what is real. For non-religious people reading this book, you may think what I am going to say will sound like I'm preaching a sermon, but I must be real about my beliefs.

I believe that real love can only come from God and His love never gets distorted or diluted. Counterfeit love is a way of manipulating someone's feelings, actions or reactions for your own benefit. Counterfeit love is all about what makes me feel good. It's time for you to find real love in your relationship with your man and how it can change their lives forever. Then, and only then, can you begin to understand unconditional love.

Unconditional Love for your man is a very different kind of love. For instance, this is when you love your man the way he is, not the way you want him to be. This means that even if he doesn't meet your expectations, you still love him the same way. Unconditional love causes you to give beyond the call or expectations of duty. Unconditional love is when you love your man without expecting anything in return. I know that this is a very hard pill for most people to swallow, but it is true. You give out of your love for your man and not out of your expected return. Unconditional love is love without trying to change your man's preferences, patterns and/or personality. This doesn't mean your man doesn't need to change, it just means that you love him the same, even if he stays just the way he is. Unconditional love is when you love your man without trying to influence him to your way.

You must understand that you might get upset or not like what your man does, but it doesn't change the love you have for him. Now this is also a challenge, unless you can distinguish between his action and the person. Many people fall short here, because the action is so closely related to the person, but you must see past the action for the sake and the good of the relationship.

A dear friend of mine told me the story of her failing relationship with her husband. She said he was a drunk, and unaffectionate towards her and abusive. She didn't like the way he was treating her or her two boys she had brought into the marriage. Things had gotten pretty bad until one day in total despair she fell to her knees and prayed to God for help. She prayed not for the situation to change, but she prayed for her husband. As the tears of frustration fell from her eyes she said she saw a vision. She saw an image of a little baby in her mind. She believed that the baby in the vision was her husband. My friend says that God let her see her husband as an innocent harmless baby and this enabled her to love him despite the hurt he had done in the past. She was able to see that the hurt from his own past as an abused child, his inability to find employment with sufficient income to take care of his family, and feelings of hopelessness was the cause of his behavior. She was able to forgive him without him asking for it and from there they were able to seek counseling to try to repair the marriage. Up until that day, she hated him, but that one prayer changed everything. Unconditional love is a powerful force.

Let's not be mistaken, artificial or secular love can also be powerful, just not nearly as powerful, nor as long lasting, as Unco nditional Love. Many people have never experienced what it is to have this kind of love in their lives. You may have unknowingly e xperienced it, but couldn't understand what was happening at the time, so let's give you some "lovology" to help you better underst and the different types of love. This time I will take a bit from my book "The Agape Doctrine" and show you how the bible uses th e word love. Is there any better place to read about unconditional love than in the bible? Most people just don't know how to apply what the bible says to their everyday living and their relationships.

There are other types of love other than unconditional. In the Greek language, which the New Testament was originally written, there were four different words that described four different types of love Eros, Phileo, Storgos and of course, Agape. Let us take a moment to define each one.

EROS– If this word sounds familiar it is, because this is where the word "e rotic" comes from. It refers to a purely carnal or physical type of love. It is not used in the Greek New Testament; however, in the Septuagint (the Greek tr anslation of the Old Testament from which Christ and the disciples quoted), i t is used in Proverbs 7:18 to refer to fleshly desires. Eros comes from God an d it enhances romance, sexual arousal and attraction. It can start a relations hip, but cannot sustain one, because it is based completely on conditions. It is often abused and misused, because of the quick, but shallow, satisfaction it provides.

PHILEO—is a verb found 24 times in the New Testament. The related P HILADELPHIA ("brotherly love") appears in the New Testament six ti mes. PHILEO describes man's love for family in Matthew 10:37, God's lov e for Jesus in John 5:20, and Christ's love for His disciple in John 13:23. T his love is not sexual, but can be a physical, warm and/or tender affection to ward something or someone. PHILEO can be emotional and expressive. It is similar to Storgos, but not the same, because it is more from the heart than n atural obligation.

STORGOS is not found in the New Testament, but the negative form of t he word (ASTORGOS) is used in Romans 1:31 and II Timothy 3:3, its meaning is "unloving." It refers to a family love and is sometimes translated " natural affection." This is the love that anyone should naturally have for their parents, children, siblings, and other family members. The bond of family blo od is strong, but not unconditional. If or when you leave or get put out of the f amily, you leave and lose the love.

AGAPE - The New Testament word for love is Agape. This is the word we base our Agape doctrine on. In order to understand The Agape Doctrine, we must first clarify the term "Agape." The word AGAPE and the noun *form of the verb is AGAPAO. The noun is used 109 times in the New Testament, and the verb is used 117 times. Agape is a Greek word in the New Testament pronounced "ag-ah'-pay." The Merriam-Webster Online Dictionary says, Agape is: 1. unselfish loyal and benevolent concern for the good of another: as (1): the fatherly concern of God for humankind (2): a person's adoration of God. Baker's Evangelical Dictionary of Biblical Theology says, "God Is Love. Agape [ajgavph], the love theme of the Bible, can only be defined by the nature of God... The theme of the entire Bible is the self-revelation of the God of love." The famous scholar and theologian, William Barclay, in his superb discussion of this word, noted that "Agape has to do with the mind: it is not simply an emotion which rises unbidden in our hearts; it is a principle by which we deliberately live." (New Testament Words, p. 21). Most of my life I have known Agape simply as the Greek word for "unconditional love;" a love that can only come from God. Now I know, while this is true, there is so much more to that truth. Even when you think of unconditional love, it's hard to comprehend how awesome it really is! It is so awesome that God has said to me that it will be the entire foundation of what I will teach for the rest of my life. Now every sermon I preach is connected in some way to the love of God.*

Well, now that you've got a bit of bible study with your relationship building, you should be ready for a little more insight on unconditional love, or let's use the word I like to use, "AGAPE." Agape love cannot be faked, but the attributes can be imitated. It will be tested and tried many times over. There will be failures, disappointments and even unmet expectations, but the love remains. This Agape love is powerful, and it will change the way you see your man. The relationship will have a different meaning when Agape is at the heart of it.

When a husband and wife love with Agape they seek ways to avoid strife and anger between them. They don't mind apologizing, because they want to resolve conflicts quickly. A relationship built on Agape is not about waiting to blame or looking for a way out of the marriage. They want to please each other and never want to hurt each other or see each other hurting. Pride, ego and uncontrolled emotions must be minimized and concern for the other person must be maximized.

You can begin practicing Agape love in your relationship, but it is not easy and takes a divine connection to be really successful. Some of the mistakes that are made by your man may produce some serious consequences, and you must continue to love him through it. There is also the possibility that your unconditional love could be taken advantage of by your man. In addition to this sometimes it takes lots of patience and more!

Read the following verse from 1 Corinthians the 13th chapter which many people like to call "The Love Chapter. *"4 Love is patient and kind. Love is not jealous or boastful or proud 5 or rude. It does not demand its own way. It is not irritable, and it keeps no record of being wronged. 6 It does not rejoice about injustice but rejoices whenever the truth wins out. 7 Love never gives up, never loses faith, is always hopeful, and endures through every circumstance."* (The Holman Christian Bible)

The above scriptures are read by many people and are used in many weddings, but for the most part it is not practiced or enforced. People don't know how. I would venture to say that without a divine connection, it is impossible.

When your love for your man is based on sex, good looks or money, it is shallow and everybody knows that sex, good looks and even money can change without warning. Most women are deeper lovers than this and their love goes beyond these surface attributes anyway. As a woman your love may be more challenged, if there is infidelity or abuse in the relationship, so let me clarify a few things.

Agape does not mean the absence of consequences for deplorable or unacceptable behavior. You cannot allow a man to beat on you, because you love him. You can't let a man have sex with other women (or men), and then come home to your bed as he pleases, because you love him. That man may need professional help and if he breaks the law, he may need rehabilitation in a correctional institution. The same bible that talks about Agape love also teaches about loving with wisdom and consequences. When there are no consequences for behavior, it will most likely be repeated in time. You do want to allow room for change and forgiveness, but you may need more than a promise from the violator. When people want to change, they will submit to whatever it takes to make those changes. If a guy says he wants to change, but he is not willing to submit to some kind of intervention or give you time and space to deal with your hurt, he probably will not change, but will just postpone the next inevitable violation. Agape is forgiving, but it is not naïve or stupid. Take care of yourself and your family. Putting yourself and your family in harm's way unnecessarily is not love; it is foolishness and dangerous.

Finally, this subject is inexhaustible. Teaching and walking in unconditional love is my passion. You can build a life around the practice as I have. It is what has brought my wife and me into the most beautiful relationship that I could have ever hoped for. We may at times disagree and have the occasional conflicts. It is not the norm, but the exception. For the most part our relationship is blissful and full of joy and excitement. She is my best friend and partner in all things. It would be easy to say that our relationship is because of who we are or our personalities match, but that would only be partly true. We all have attributes that can make us compatible to some degree with another human being, but my wife and I had some major issues that were potential problems for a marriage. I was a very dominate, unorganized, overbearing, fast-paced, risk-taking, entrepreneur. My wife is a quiet, stability-seeking, slow-moving, 9 to 5 career worker. It was the revelation and practice of Agape that sealed or relationship and made it what it is today.

Let me end this very important chapter with a post from

the website of Harold W. Becker, the author of the book, *Unconditional Love -An Unlimited Way of Being:*

> *"Unconditional Love is a dynamic and powerful energy that lifts us through the most difficult times. It is available at any moment by turning our attention to it and using its wonderful potential to free us from our limitations. It requires practice and intent to allow this energy to fully permeate our daily experience. It begins with ourselves, for without self-love, we cannot know what true love can be. In loving ourselves, we allow the feeling to generate within us and then we can share it to everyone and everything around us! That which we send out, returns to us in greater measure. If you have not thought about how you feel towards yourself, physically, mentally, and emotionally, or spiritually, we invite you to do so now. Begin the journey that changes everything. Begin the journey of unconditional love..."*

NINETEEN

Men Love Good Mommies
(but they don't marry them)

We all know that a man's first love is his mother (as we pointed out in our introduction of this book). It is also a fact that when men have good perceptions of their mother's they usually look for women with the same good traits. It doesn't matter if that person is their true biological mother or not such as a grandmother, stepmothers or any other surrogate mother. The man is attached to the nurturing aspects of the mother/son relationship. Most men, who have healthy and positive relationships with the moms in their lives, find themselves almost magnetically drawn to those same nurturing women in romantic relationships as they grow older.

There is a theory created and made popular by Sigmund Freud, also known as the father of psychology, called the *Oedipal Complex*. By definition the *Oedipal Complex* is a term used in his theory of psychosexual stages of development to describe a boy's feelings of desire for his mother and jealously and anger towards his father. The position is that essentially, a boy feels like he is in competition with his father for possession of his mother. He views his father as a rival for her attention and affections, and subconsciously wishes to possess his mother and replace his father. There is much debate over this theory, but I think that Freud is on to something. MEN LOVE A GOOD MOMMY!

My own mother, Ann Pearson, is a wonderful and caring person whom I just adore. She is 75 years old and still my favorite person in the world. She is fun with a witty sense of humor, wise with good instincts and will give you the shirt off of her own back just to help you. I am almost 54 years old now and in good health, but even today if I go to visit her, she will offer to cook me a meal and grab her cane on the way to the kitchen before I can answer. I love these traits about my mother and yes I married a woman with these exact same traits. I have been in relationships with other women over the years and if physical attractiveness was the thing that drew me to them, but they didn't have my mother's attributes the relationship was short lived.

With this said, you must understand that although a man may be drawn to your "mommy-ness" there is another side of the mommy that men hate. Most men hate too much "mothering." My definition of mothering is when a woman watches over her husband as if she must protect him from himself. Grown men, like me, may love their mothers, but too much mothering is annoying and unhealthy. This is why men love good mommies to take care of them, but they don't normally want to be married to them.

My point is that a touch of a good mother here and there is great, but too much mothering can be very dangerous. I found an interesting article online that seems to agree with my position on this often misunderstood and ignored subject, it is entitled:

Do You Mommy Your Husband?

April 30, 2008 | By Sarah Jio

Kristen Rounds, 26, admits that she's a little gaga over her man. "I'm like his mommy," the Monterey Park, California, resident says with a laugh about her fiancé, a first-year medical student. Case in point: She picks out his clothes before they go out, styles his hair, makes his lunches (complete with "I love you" notes inside) and takes it upon herself to apply the toothpaste before handing him his toothbrush each night.

And then there's bathing. "When he's in the shower, he calls me in to wash his back," says Rounds, a publicist.
Over-the-top behavior? Rounds says no way. "He loves to be taken care of."

It's a scenario familiar to many relationship experts, who say that first comes love, then comes marriage, and then comes the husband in the baby carriage.

Nurturing gene on overdrive

Women find themselves mothering their husbands because of societal pressures to be the ultimate woman, says Pepper Schwartz, a sociology professor at the University of Washington in Seattle. "We've been taught that the way to show love is to do for others," she says. And, according to Schwartz, some women believe that the more they nurture, the better a woman they are. "I was at a dinner party once," she says, "and I watched a woman lean over and start cutting up her husband's meat."

A bad idea? "It can work for some people," says Les Parrott, a clinical psychologist, an author on marriage and relationship topics, and a professor at Seattle Pacific University. He describes one couple he knows: "She packs his suitcase for him and takes care of him like a little kid. But it works for them." Even so, Parrott and other experts are quick to point out that while a certain amount of nurturing is harmless, it can escalate and lead to relationship trouble. "First you're tucking in his shirt," Schwartz says, "then you're wiping his mouth, and at some point, it's going to become a problem."

It was a problem for New York City resident Linda Franklin's marriage. "As a woman who mothered her husband for too many years, I can report it's about the worst thing a woman can do," says Franklin, 55, a writer and lifestyle coach for female baby boomers. "It makes your man lazy, unwilling to be proactive in his own health care and for the most part a boy who refuses to grow up. It took me a long time to understand you can be compassionate and loving without being smothering and controlling." Franklin says she resisted the urge to mother her husband so much, and the result has been a happier marriage.

To look even deeper into how men feel when there is too much mothering, we have to see the negative side of his feelings when he feels he is married to his mother. The man will feel like his woman is watching his every move and to a grown man that translates into distrust in his mind. The more insecure you as a woman are the more your man will feel how much you don't trust him. If he is a human being (which I hope he is), he will make mistakes on occasion. While mommy may chalk it up as the process of growing up; an insecure wife may have problems with letting those mistakes go and tend to keep mental records of them. The insecurity can cause them to process many of those mistakes as personal and purposed and they may not be either. When a person processes an action of another person as being personally against them, it goes much deeper than it does than being processed as a random mistake. This makes it much harder to let go. Mothering sees the need to correct and punish when your man makes a mistake. From here we get the picture of the nagging wife shaking her finger at her husband or the man pleading his case in front of the judge.

I presented the preceding cartoon not to suggest or advocate any violence, but to show what the effects of mothering your husband too much could produce.

Now, for a final word about too much mothering. Despite Freud's *Oedipal Complex* theory that sons are jealous of their father's relationship with their mother, normal men don't want to have sexual relationships with the mother. This should be very important for you as a woman to know. If you create a "mothering" image of yourself to your husband, it may interfere with his ability or desire to be sexual with you. It may sound crazy, but remember, men are very visual when it comes down to sexual arousal. Too much of the "mother connection" in the relationship may conflict with the imagery he needs of you to become sexually aroused. He needs to see you as his sexy wife and lover, not his nurturing mother.

This can cause big problems for you in the bedroom. It may cause him to rely on pornography or some other visualization techniques to arouse him. He is not wired like you and he needs much more than love and emotion to be sexually aroused. This does not necessarily mean that he does not love you or does not want to be with you sexually. It may mean that he could be having difficulty focusing on the sex if his subconscious is preoccupied with trying not to see you as a mother to him. There could be a mental war going on and he just cannot break through. If the picture in his head of the nagging wife in our cartoon translates into a nagging critical mother, you may never get the affection you want out of him or anything else for that matter!

Even a woman who is a good mother to her children must be careful not to bring that mommy too deep into the bedroom. It too can remind him of his mother so much so that he begins to see you as her instead of his wife. There are multiple facets to you as a woman. You may be a mother but that cannot dominate the relationship too much. He needs you to be his bride, his girlfriend, his mysterious mistress, his partner, his fantasy, his confidante and then he needs you to be you, that woman he fell in love with! You may say, "I don't have time to be all of those things!" Then it may be time to organize your life better. True, after you have a child much of your time goes into that and if you're working and trying to keep the home in order, it's hard or even at times impossible to also be a virtual runway model at home. So you must try to organize your time the best that you can. Here are a couple of tips:

Make a Plan That Works For You. "Fail to plan, plan to fail." You have to determine that you will not just let the events of the day run you. Set something in place that is manageable, but not so rigid that you set yourself up for failure.

Evaluate and Present Yourself. Look at where you are now and where you want to be. You may want to insert school into your plan or a career goal. Ask yourself about the future affects from the life you are planning. Will it make you happier? Will it bring you closer to your family? Will you regret your plan of today later?

Sort Out the Duties. If it is just you and your husband and you are both working, you should look at all of your household chores and determine who will be responsible for what chores. Together agree to share the responsibilities of keeping things in order. This should give you more time to do your runway modeling for him and have some "me time" for you.

Write the Plan Down. Make a calendar, appointment schedule in your phone or day timer. Put your plan and schedule down somewhere that is visible and accessible for both of you or the whole family. There will be times when the plan may need to be adjusted, but make sure everyone knows about it when that happens.

Follow Up. Keep up on the progress of the plans and goals of the household. Create events such as a pizza night or special dinners to discuss additions, violations and adjustments that need to be made. In other words create a pleasant environment for these family business meetings, if you have to deal with issues with the plan. If the issues are more serious, you may have to have a special "Call Meeting" for certain things.

Separate Home from Work. Unless you work at home do everything you can to make your home environment a get-away from your job(s). This means it may be okay to have light discussion about the job, but don't bring the stress, culture and complexities from work into the life of your family.

Enjoy Being a Family! If it's just two of you or twelve, put some fun time and pleasure in your plan. It may be as simple as a trip to the library or a walk in the park. It could be a high school football game or the NBA playoffs, whatever your time and budget will allow. You may have to make time and budget, if possible, but do something that can generate some laughter and relaxation.

These tips can help bring some balance into what could be an otherwise life of pressure, criticism and boredom for both you and your man.

BUT WHAT ABOUT MY CONCERNS! There may be a legitimate reason for your nagging, but you need to learn something I heard a long time ago, *"You can catch more flies with sugar than with vinegar!"*

Mothering, nagging, complaining, comparing, and/or criticizing will never win your husband's affection. If you think you are doing these things, you are also probably unhappy and wishing for a better relationship. I don't blame you, but I'm pretty sure that a big portion of the blame should be put on the behavior that you probably learned or developed.

If you do have concerns that need to be addressed take a few things into consideration first:

- Is this the right time and/or place?
- Is the issue really important?
- Is it worth bringing up?
- Can you bringing it up help to fix it?
- Can it be fixed or are you just venting?
- Are you handling it like a wife or a mother?
- Are you being demanding?
- Are you nagging?

Let me close this chapter with these two famous quotes from the bible:

Proverbs 21:9 ESV
It is better to live in a corner of the housetop than in a house shared with a quarrelsome wife.

Proverbs 21:19 ESV
It is better to live in a desert land than with a quarrelsome and fretful woman.

TWENTY

Manage That Money

It seems to be common knowledge that most women in our country love to shop. I have heard some women call it "retail therapy." I am pretty fortunate. My wife loves to shop, but she loves second hand stores, like Goodwill and Savers (what a wonderful woman)! She will spend hours going from store to store; she walks out with big bags full of all kinds of stuff. Some things are great deals and exactly what we needed and some things are what I call "just for the moment." The only problem I have getting rid of the stuff she might only keep it for a "moment" time since it's so cheap.

Money is a big issue for many couples. Across the country counselors are mediators for more arguments, separations, fights and divorces over money than with any other issue. Sometimes it's not about being money-less, because having money can be just as big of a problem as not having money. I could just cut and paste chapter 18 from my earlier book, *20 ½*

Ways for a Man to Love His Woman, entitled *Money Matters With Your Woman,* but men and women do spend differently.

When women shop they want to have more options and a variety of things to choose from and to be able to experience them internally. Their shopping seems almost spiritual, touching each item, feeling and comparing textures and colors. Men are much different. A man usually knows exactly what he wants; the color, style and other properties before he ever walks in the store. When I shop I don't need a salesman, just clearly posted signs, so I can find what I'm looking for and a cash register for my purchase.

There are some ideas from that book that I will bring up again in this book as the information is very important and you and your man need to be aware of the danger that financial mismanagement could cause.

Please don't take this subject lightly, because money issues have a way of affecting us differently than anything else. It catches most of us off guard. Most of us grow up believing that when we get married, what's yours is mine and what's mine is yours. There is no separation of assets. Some of us have even taken premarital classes to prepare us for some of these issues, but there are not many classes on subjects like:

1. I have a whole lot more; you have a whole lot less.
2. I'm a good money manager; you're not.
3. I have triple "A" credit; you have triple "F" credit.
4. I believe in saving; you believe in spending.
5. I shop when I'm depressed; you get depressed when I shop.
6. I manage my bills; your bills manage you.
7. I've worked on the same job for ten years; you've worked ten jobs in one year.
8. I'm the investor and you're the "investee."

9. I think my ship of good fortune sank when you climb
    ed on board.

For some of you, none of the above scenarios apply to you or your man, but for others, many, if not all, of these thoughts have often crossed your mind.

Simply put, some people are terrible at managing money. If your man is the kind of guy who let's money run through his fingers like water, don't badger him with insults and derogatory conclusions. Use tact and love and attempt to suggest a change. For instance, rather than telling him how terrible of a job he has done - I recommend you suggest that he may be too busy to take care of managing the money and that you are more than willing to help him out. Let him know that you have more time or can rearrange your schedule to be more helpful. The insults will only make him defensive and less cooperative.

Depending on the relationship you have with your man dealing with money could be easier than you think. As a woman, you first must learn how to handle your money properly before you can do it in a relationship with a man. Learning how to adhere to a budget, avoid denial of the difficult financial issues and excessive spending is essential to proper management. Only after that can you have the correct pieces to begin allocating the funds in a home with a husband and possibly children reasonably. This brings me to the issue of over-spending.

I love researching the internet for research to find good articles and I found a very great article the other day written by Jodi Helmer that described the top 8 reasons why we overspend. See if any of this fits your situation:

1. You spend more when paying with plastic. (I think m

ost of us know this.) This is due to the fact that we st op focusing on the price and more on the item we wa nt to buy; we're willing to pay more with a credit card, than if we had to pay cash.

2. When music is playing you're inclined to spend more. Studies have shown that music makes you exercise be tter and also increases your motivation to spend.

3. Buying in bulk can cause you to spend more. If you b uy a bunch of something (like 50 rolls of toilet paper) it throws your monthly budgeting out of whack and y ou're likely to use up the product more quickly knowi ng there's lots more available.

4. Dieting can cause you to spend more on other things. If you're deprived in one area you're more likely to im pulse spend in another.

5. Tracking exact costs. Your eyes might be tracking pur chases to the penny, but research shows that you mig ht lose sight of the total amount you're spending. (Th e old "You can't see the forest for the trees" problem.)

6. Buying clearance items. They look really cheap, but yo u probably don't need them; you buy "just in case" an d overspend.

7. Shopping without a list is one of the most mentioned "no-no's. The reason is obvious, I think.

8. Falling for price tactics. Everything is relative. If you g o to a restaurant where the menu has a $100 burger a nd a $50 steak, you will think the burger price is crazy, but the steak price almost seems reasonable.

It is amazing when we consider how and why we actually spend as much as we do. "Impulse" is our worst enemy when it comes down to spending and if you are a highly emotional woman you may find yourself with house full of items you don't need and don't even want after some time has passed and the impulse has diminished.

Nobody wants to see their hard earned money squandered or wasted away. Your man may be the type of guy who has no sympathy for your "retail therapy" need. Many men feel trapped by a woman who feels they must have their nails and their hair done every week or they have a closet full of clothes and shoes, but say they have nothing to wear. For a man this might be very frustrating to deal with and it can put a tremendous strain on your relationship, if it is not controlled properly.

This next section is straight from my previous book *20 ½ Ways for a Man to Love His Woman*. Although I wrote this next part for a man to read, both men and women can benefit from these readings and I hope you will appreciate the following advice:

Whether we admit it or not, finances have come up in many of the conversations of the most loving partners. It is not very easy to talk about, because it is one of those things that could remain the same after marriage. You made money before you got married and you still can make money now. It was yours before you got married and it's still yours. You just agree to use it for the common good of the household.

In our Western culture we believe the man is supposed to support his wife and family, but it just doesn't always happen like that. Some women are better educated than their husbands. This can be a challenge for either or both of them.

Prior to marriage, your woman may have been doing fine without your help and you may have been fine without hers. Now you have to include your mate in the financial decisions even though you feel you are fully capable of making it without her help. In addition to this, depending on what state you are in, you now have to share the responsibility of whatever debts you create after you marry.

Finances in a marriage can be a big problem, no matter how much in love the couple may be. Here are few reasons why finances can cause a rift in good marriages:

1. **Poor management skills**. If a person never learns to manage resources, he will always find himself coming up short. It doesn't matter if it is money, gas for the car, or hours in the day. The ability to manage doesn't come automatically. Managing resources is a skill that must be learned. Some people are taught while growing up and others learn by trial and error. It doesn't always mean that the person is bad, because they are a poor manager. Some manage well; some do other things well. Very few classes teach adults how to manage their resources. A patient spouse can do wonders for a person who realizes that he/she may have problems in that area. In fact, if you have a spouse that doesn't handle the money very well and is honest enough to admit it, you have a jewel that many people wish they had. If he really wants to try to manage the money, give him a chance. If she asks for it, pay attention to what's going on. When there have been enough indications of failure such as returned checks, shut off notices and phone calls from creditors, then it's time to take action.

2. **The need to be in control**. Some people just need to be in control. They may know they have a

problem managing the finances, but they cannot give up control. They have an excuse for every blunder they make. This person is a little harder to deal with, because pride is a part of the problem. You still have to take action or you may be part of the homeless population and soon. Be smart, here's an approach you can take. "You were right. I should start taking some of this responsibility off of you." If your woman feels overwhelmed, you may want to say something like this, "You work so hard. How could I expect you to manage the finances too? I'm not being very fair to you. If you still want me to, I'll do the family banking...but I'll need your help, please." Suggest as many ways as possible that you can work together. There's also a possibility that trust has been broken in the past. If you are the one who broke her trust, be patient, because you will have to earn her trust again. You will never earn her trust, if you are doing the same things you did that caused you to lost it.

3. **Need for formal education**. Take classes and read books on financial management together. This can be a tremendous help. First make sure the class instructor is fair-minded. The last thing you need is a male chauvinist or a feminist teaching from a biased perspective. Then take a class and share ideas throughout the class. I found it is better when your classmates don't know that you are husband and wife. You get a better, more open response from the class as a whole. They see you as just two more classmates (Plus, it's exciting watching people trying to date your spouse, if you're secure enough to handle it. I saw it as a compliment to my good taste).

4. **Listen to your woman's advice.** Talk about your spending habits. Learn to communicate before you make major purchases. If your woman doesn't think it's a good idea, don't fight it. Instead have a peaceful discussion, weighing the pros and the cons. If emotions are too high at the moment, wait 24 hours and then bring it up again. Anytime you can't make a decision together, it's best to wait or not do it at all. Even if you want to surprise your mate with something, save up for it or just make sure it's not going to cause a major problem at home. Try to have a little savings anyway, in case there is an unbeatable once in a lifetime sale, but don't be fooled -- unbeatable once in a lifetime sales happen every day.

If you are having financial problems and you are reading this book with your woman, stop playing games and throwing away your hard-earned money. The cost of bounced checks, late fees, reconnection notices and such can really add up! If you are not doing well handling the money for whatever reason, give your woman a chance at it. Whatever the situation may be, both of you should be working together anyway.

If you have a good relationship, don't let money or the lack of it ruin it. Learn to please your lover when the bills are paid or if they're all behind. Accept the fact that the money and your relationship are two different things. It is very hard for couples to be good lovers when they are stressed out about money issues.

If you make a mistake with the money (or with anything else), humbly apologize. Do this from your heart not out of obligation, but because you are really sorry for any embarrassment and inconvenience you may have caused. It's better to admit an oversight with a sincere apology than to say nothing at all, hoping it will be soon forgotten.

Money is a sensitive issue in a marriage; but with a few adjustments in attitude and with the addition of a few management skills, your relationship can still be pleasing. Just keep at the forefront that your relationship or your own personal value should never be defined by how much money you have or don't have. One day my wife and I were going through a rough financial phase and I told her we may have to down-size and make some changes. She looked at me and said," it doesn't matter what we have to do or give up. As long as I'm with you I'll be happy." When she said that it almost brought tears to my eyes and right then and there I knew that I was more important to her than any of the "stuff" we had acquired

Your "stuff" may come and go. You may go through tough times and have some bad days. Learn how to love each other during the dark days and you'll appreciate better the good times. Money can make you or break you, but only if you let it. Don't give your money that much power!

An old proverb says, *"If you want to feel rich, just count the things you have that money can't buy."*

These excerpts from my book have helped many men to see where they went wrong when it came to money management with their women and I do hope you picked up on the key issue, which is don't let your money rule you!

Please take all of that you read in this chapter to heart. Although I know many women who are great at financial management, few women can resist the lure of good deal. You may need to make some drastic changes in the way you currently operate financially, but it is worth it, if it helps to build up your relationship with your man.

TWENTY AND A HALF

Personal Prostitute Training

This chapter is only number at ½ because if you get the other things right this part comes very easy and can take half the time to master. Here we talk about sexual enjoyment. Some of you women are insulted by this chapter title, but some of you know exactly what this means and why I say it. First off this does not mean that you should start charging your husband for sex or stand out on the street corner for him. Now that we have that out of the way, let's get down to business. It has been said that prostitution is the oldest profession on the earth and I wouldn't doubt that. What is it that makes a man go out and pick up a complete stranger, take her to some undisclosed location and pay her to have sex with him? Many women would answer and say, "Because he's a dog and can't control his sexual urges." It would be simple if that's all it was, but this is far from the truth.

There are trampy street whores who take any dollar they can get for sexual acts, but that is not who I am referring to now. The prostitute who is paid well and in high demand is a professional at knowing how to please the man she is with, but this goes beyond sexual intercourse. She must detect and meet his needs. This woman is rarely with a man who simply wants to "get laid." This woman is skilled at helping him to open up and share his wildest fantasy and deepest needs. She removes all fears he may have and if the price is right she takes him to where ever his mind wants to go.

She makes him feel that he is the best man she is ever been with, although he knows that she tells that to every customer who walks in the door. She makes him feel whatever he needs to feel at that time, because she knows that her pay and his return is based on him being completely satisfied. She totally understands her role and knows that she must play it well. I am not saying that a woman should subject herself to the demeaning task of just using her body for her husband's pleasure alone. I'm saying that if a wife understands that her husband's needs are for more than a sexual release she can sexually please him and herself at the same time. Some prostitutes have been paid big dollars just to listen to a man who needs a friend and can't find that in his own wife. Some men go to prostitutes, because his wife just doesn't understand how a man thinks or feels sexually. Let's deal with that. This next section is for mature audiences only!

TIPS ON SATISFYING YOUR MAN SEXUALLY

1. When he's ready, he's ready! Most men hate it when a wo man wants to talk when he is ready to have sex and forepl ay can be frustrating too. Women must understand that a man's body is not like hers. I don't just mean the obvious appearance issue, but in functionality. A man cannot have sex without an erection and when it happens, he is ready! His body functions must be respected! He doesn't have t o build up to it like a woman does. He can see one sexual

thing, have a single sexual thought or get one single little s exual touch and in most cases his body will instantly resp ond. Women you must understand that the erection is not a precursor to sex; to a man it is the sex! Foreplay happen s mentally and it can happen in about 10 to 20 seconds (d epending on age and/or physical conditioning)! When he has an erection he is ready to perform sexually at that mo ment…not later. After that point the urge builds up quick ly and he is ready to deliver his seed or ejaculate. The sex drive is very strong and a man usually has one thing as his objective which is ejaculation. Although this may be sexua lly frustrating for you, he has little to do with this because he's was created this way. Men can learn to control this, b ut this is where some women who don't have a clue as to how to handle this get frustrated. You may need the help of a trained sex therapist or get some self-help material to work through this issue. As men mature they eventually l earn the benefit of slowing down and actual enjoying the person who they are having sex with over the sexual act it self. I say again, "eventually!"

2. Men are visual. If you are ashamed of your body or you fe el too shy to show it, you have a major chance of loosing him to pornography, a prostitute or another woman. As h orrible as this may sound, this is a fact ladies. But it is also a fact that if a woman knows how to use her body to visu ally entice and stimulate her man "size doesn't always mat ter." Most men are excited about the body parts first and everything else follows. Tap into what visually turns your man on about you. Show it to him. Give him a peek when he least expects it. Phone sex used to be very popular. It g

ave the hearer a visual in their minds even when the perso
n was miles away. Don't be afraid of being the main thou
ght in your husband's mind. Create a sexy picture in his m
ind with your creative verbal skills. In other words "Be as
freely graphic as you possibly can be!"

3. You have what it takes. God gave you a body that will attr
   act the right man to you and it is up to you to keep yourse
   lf attractive for him, but that doesn't mean you have to be
   skin and bones to do it. You are who you are. Men like th
   e shape of hips. Bend over in front of that TV sometimes
   and give him a snap shot of what is his (not during the pla
   yoffs, that could be dangerous). Most men are more excit
   ed about the size and shape of your nipples than they are
   the size of your breasts, so don't be so quick to get that e
   nlargement. Be proud of your sexual body parts more tha
   n   what   size   dress   you   wear.

4. Connect to the man who likes your body type. (This is a b
   efore marriage tip.) Some men like big breasts, but some
   don't. Some like big butts and others like small ones. Men
   are different and different men like different things about
   their particular woman. Yes, your body does change over
   the years, but do what you can to be what your husband e
   njoys. His body is changing too.

5. Some men enjoy fetishes, so be prepared for sexual creati
   vity and make your relationship with him open enough w
   here he can express himself with you sexually any way he
   wants to. As I said in #2 many men love to hear you talk
   about sex. Some folks call it "dirty talk." Don't be ashame

d to tell him how you like it, when you like it, where you li ke it and how often you like it. Help keep the stimulation high by building up with him as you talk about your enjoy ment. He wants to know he's the best (please don't comp are him with others, it may backfire). He wants to know h ow good he makes you feel. Compliment him, his muscle s, his strength, the size of his penis, the way he moves (an y   and   all   that   apply).

6. Experiment. Be willing to try something new. Don't be so quick to say what you won't like or that you tried that bef ore. Allow your man to feel that he can do anything with you. It may not be as pleasurable to you, but it may thrill him. I do advise against multiple partners, perversion and sex outside the marriage. If something hurts or is uncomf ortable gently let him know it. In a case like that, it would be a good idea, if you were the one to suggest something else (most men really love this) rather than spending too much time talking about why you don't like doing the oth er act. There are plenty of sexual aids available like books and videos (they aren't all porn) that have many creative i deas   that   you   could   try.

7. Have fun! Enjoy your husband sexually. Make your time t ogether special. Don't complain about being tired or havi ng the infamous "headache." Be careful not to be so serio us or demanding. Relax and laugh a little. Try some sexual pet names. Try some sex games and some sex toys. Look forward to fun that helps to release tension and stress. Jus t make sure you don't get distracted from the main point. Good sex!

8. Be spontaneous! Don't always plan when, how where and etc. You and your husband should have sex any time you can and anywhere you can. Remember the early days of y our marriage! You may be older and smarter, but just thin k how your husband would feel if one Saturday you were driving down the street together and you said, "Honey let' s get a room in that hotel I want to make love to you now!" Walk in the room naked in the middle of the day and say, "I just need a 2 minute breast massage…would you mind?" Show up at his office with a long coat on and sexy lingeri e underneath. Close the door give him a peek and say, "I need you to come home as quick as possible our bed is o n fire and I need you to put it out!" Need I say more?

9. Use technology. Send him a sexy text message or an email. Tell him you miss him or you want him. Try some sexy c ode words or phrases only the two of you know. You sho uld be careful about computers on his job, but remember, he is your husband. If you get caught it may be a little em barrassing, but it's not illegal. It might be a little turn-on, i f you did get caught. I would caution against sending nud e pictures of each other. Those pictures could get circulat ed all over the internet and in some states they are consid ered pornography.

10. Public Play. Sometimes it's nice to sneak a few touches an d feels when you're out in public. Nothing is sexier than t wo people in love who just can't keep their hands off of e ach other. Be discrete and look out for kids. I'm not talki ng about flashing or fondling just a pat on the butt or a p

urposed, but discrete push of his pouch.

11. The bedroom. The ultimate turn on is the personal bedro om strip show and lap dance. The point here is to take yo ur time to make him feel that he never has to go anywher e, but with you to have all his one on one sexual needs sat isfied. Make that bedroom into a place where the two of y ou have the best of times. Teach the kids that they must a lways knock and after two knocks you are not available, s o stop knocking.

12. You're never too old! As you get older the libido can lesse n and the erections can be more difficult to maintain. Thi s does not mean to shut down the sex. You may need to be more creative. You need more manual stimulation or s ome other sexual aids like medication, gels, etc. Women, when your sex drive is slowing down your husband may s till need and want to make love to you. Ask him how he f eels from time to time, even if you don't feel like it and pl ease be willing to comply. Tell him what you need. Don't let your age destroy your sex life. Do it as long as you can!

BONUS TIPS FOR COUPLES

Just a few final tips you want to always remember throughout your lifetime together as lovers.

♥ **Always support each other's positive efforts**, even if you d iffer on methodology.

♥ **Learn how to compliment first, then cautiously construc tively criticize if you must criticize at all.** Sometimes the ti ming is not right for your personal opinions.

♥ **Always try to be as gentle and kind to each other as poss ible, especially when you're angry.** Remember, "You catc h more flies with sugar than with vinegar."

♥ **Give a compliment, and say "I love you" at least once a day.** Don't think to yourself, "Oh, they know it." The point is in you saying it and in them hearing it from you.

♥ **Never abuse your lover or stay in an abusive situation.** T here is no gain in that kind of pain.

♥ **The grass may look greener on the other side.** Instead of going to the other side, try mowing and watering your own gr ass first.

♥ **Have an open heart for forgiveness.** Don't be so quick to j udge your lover. We all make mistakes and need forgiveness at some time.

♥ **A third objective party might be helpful sometimes**. Re member there are three sides to every story - your side, their s ide and what really happened.

♥ **Partner with your partner!** Don't just be a couple, but be a partnership.

♥ **Don't badger your lover over an issue**. Sometimes it's best to do what the old song says, "Let it be."

EPILOGUE

Well, these are my final words as I close this powerful and exciting book written just with you in mind. There is much to learn and discover as you venture deeper into having the best relationship possible. If there was one word that best describes what I have said to you in this book, it would be, "listen." Listen carefully to what your man says. Listen to his wants and needs. Don't pass it off as unimportant. Many men have problems expressing their true feelings and really need to have a woman who will hear them. Here is a nice quote that expresses this thought well,

"A man is already halfway in love with any woman who listens to him."

Brenda Francis

You have been given the best advice I can possibly give you! I pray that you seriously consider everything I have offered you with an open mind. Something may not fit your particular situation exactly as I have presented it and you may need to make some minor adjustments. Read the book more than once and read it with your man. I'm sure his reaction will affirm what you have read here. Now, go on and implement the new tactics, put to good use the information and practice until you perfect these 20 ½ Ways to Please Your Man (and keep him)! God Bless You!

Dr. Rodney Pearson

ABOUT THE AUTHOR

Dr. Rodney Pearson is a teacher, minister, singer, playwright, musician, a long-time community activist in ministry and relationship coach. For over 30 years Dr. Pearson has served as a senior pastor and planted six churches while operating in the office of an Apostle of Jesus Christ. Dr. Pearson trains leaders, conducts seminars and workshops nationally on the subject of relationships, team building and conflict resolution.

Dr. Rodney Pearson is also a former professor at the Southern C alifornia School of Ministry where he received his Masters in Mini stry degree. Dr. Pearson received his Associate of Arts (psycholo gy major) from San Bernardino Community College in California, a Bachelors of Science a Master's in professional counseling from Grand Canyon University. He also attended Fuller Seminary in P asadena, California and received his Doctorate of Ministry from Living Word Bible College.

Dr. Pearson has received several awards and commendations for his community work. He is the founder of the Love on Fire Chur ch, an exciting and powerful ministry near Phoenix, Arizona, whe re the gospel of unconditional love is taught and practiced regular ly.

Dr. Rodney Pearson and his dear wife, Trenna, are available for workshops, seminars and other speaking engagements!

Other Great Books
By Dr. Rodney Pearson

The Agape Doctrine
Exposing Manipulation
Significantly Single
20 ½ Ways for a Man to Love His Woman
The Power of the Process
10 Short Steps to Managing Conflict
100 Proverbs of Love
7 Sacred Sins (a fiction novel)

For More Information on these books:

www.youarelovedpublishing.com

www.amazon.com

These books can also be ordered from any
bookstore across the nation and beyond!